ON THE ORIGINAL INHABITANTS OF BHARATAVARSA OR INDIA

THE DRAVIDIANS

ON THE ORIGINAL INHABITANTS OF BHARATAVARSA OR INDIA

THE DRAVIDIANS

GUSTAV OPPERT

GYAN

Published by

Gyan Publishing House
5, Ansari Road
Daryaganj, New Delhi-110002
Phone: 011-47034999, 9811692060
E-mail: books@gyanbooks.com

Distribution Network
gyanbooks.com
India, USA, Canada, UK, Australia, France

ISBN : 978-81-212-3337-8 (PB)
First Published, 1888

2nd Impression 2020

Printed at: Gyan Press, Delhi.

On The original Inhabitants of Bharatavarsa or India
The Dravidians
Author: Gustav Oppert

PREFACE TO PART I.

The work, of which this treatise is the first part, has been written to prove, mainly on philological grounds, the antiquity and expansion of the Gauda-Dravidian race in India. This first part is devoted to its Dravidian branch.

The second part will treat of the Gaudians, and in the third will be considered the conclusions which may be deduced from the two preceding.

An appendix will contain the numerous geographical names scattered over India, which indicate the presence of the Gauda-Dravidian race.

In pursuing the ramifications of the Dravidian population throughout the peninsula, I hope I have been able to point out the connection existing between several tribes, apparently widely different from each other. I have tried thus to identify the so-called Pariahs of Southern India with the old Dravidian mountaineers and to establish their relationship to the Bhārs, Brahuis, Mhārs, Mahārs, Pahārias, Paravārī, Pāradas and others; all these tribes forming, as it were, the first layer of the ancient Dravidian stratum. In addition to this I trust I have shown that all such different tribes as the Mallas, Pallas, Pallavas, Ballas, Bhillas and others are one and all offshoots of the Dravidian race, the derivation of whose name from *Tirumala*, as proposed by me, must, if established, also add some strength to my theory. Moreover I have endeavoured to demonstrate how much that is now considered Aryan in name and in origin must be regarded as originally Dravidian.

The various principal Dravidian tribes who live scattered over the length and breadth of the vast Indian continent are, in order to establish their mutual kindredship, separately introduced into this discussion. This method may create in the minds of some readers an impression that the several topics are somewhat disconnected, but the necessity for this arrangement will become manifest in the continuation of this treatise.

Where there is so much room for conjecture, it is easy enough, of course, to fall into error, and I shall be prepared to be told that many of my conclusions are erroneous and the hypotheses on which they are built fanciful. But though much of what I have written may be shown to be untenable, I shall yet be satisfied if, in the main, I establish my contention, and I shall deem myself amply repaid for my labour if I succeed in any degree in restoring the Dravidian to those rights and honours of which he has so long been deprived.

My errors, too, may not be without use, if, like stranded vessels, they serve to direct the explorer, warning him away from those shoals and rocks that beset the enquirer in his search after truth.

System of Transliteration.

k, kh, g, gh, ṅ, ḥ, h, a, ā.
c, ch, j, jh, ñ, ś, y, i, ī, e,[1] ē, ai.
ṭ, ṭh, ḍ, ḍh, ṇ, ṣ, r, ṛ, ṝ
t, th, d, dh, n, s, l, ḷ, ḹ.
p, ph, b, bh, m, ḥ, v, u, ū, o[1], ō, au.
Anusvāra ṁ; ṟ, ḻ, ḻ, are peculiar to the Dravidian languages.

[1] Used in Dravidian languages.

CONTENTS.

INTRODUCTION.

CHAPTER I.

PART I.

THE DRAVIDIANS.

CHAPTER II.

CHAPTER III.

CHAPTER IV.

CHAPTER V.

CHAPTER VI.

On the Original Inhabitants of Bharatavarṣa or India.

INTRODUCTION.

CHAPTER I.

General Remarks.

No one who undertakes to study the ancient history of India can fail to be impressed by the scantiness of the material at his disposal. In fact such an undertaking would soon appear to be futile, were he to depend solely on Indian accounts and records. Fortunately, however, we possess some writings of foreigners who visited India; and their reports of what they actually saw during their stay in this country, and of what they were able to gather from trustworthy sources, furnish us with materials of a sufficiently reliable character. If we except Kashmir and Ceylon, regarding the latter as belonging to India, no part of India possesses anything like a continuous historical record. The preponderance of caste and the social prejudices it creates are disabilities such as no Hindu who wishes to relate the history of his country can entirely overcome. The natives of India have, as a rule, little sympathy with people outside their own class, and when it is believed that persons belonging to the highest caste can by their piety ensure final beatitude, if they simply remember and revere the memory of their three immediate predecessors—father, grandfather, and great grandfather—we need not wonder at the apathy displayed towards history by them and by others who are beneath them in the social scale.

*

Yet, if the study of Indian history has up to now not proved interesting to the Hindus themselves—and there exist many good reasons why this has been and is still the case—this fact need not discourage foreigners, who are interested in this subject, from pursuing it.

It is true no doubt that the results which have been obtained from decipherings and archæological researches in India, must appear insignificant when compared with what has been achieved elsewhere in the same fields. Still, there is no need to despair of final success, for our knowledge and material are daily increasing, though Indian history at present, becomes interesting only when it throws light on the communal, legal and social conditions of the people, or on their intercourse and relation with foreigners.

Owing to the meagreness and often to the untrustworthiness of the historical material, an Indian historian must be continually on the look-out for new tracks in which to pursue his researches. The task of a scientific historian is difficult in itself, but it is made still more so, if a scholar is anxious to make original researches and strike out for himself a new path in Indian history, as, in addition to other qualifications, he must be a linguist possessing some knowledge of the language of the people into whose past he is inquiring.

The limited number of Indian historical records, including architectural, palæographical, numismatic and similar antiquities, compels a student of Indian history to draw within his range subjects other than those usually regarded as strictly historical, *e.g.*, the names of nations and individuals, of countries and towns, of mountains and rivers, and such other topics, in which he believes that historical relics lie concealed.

I have selected as the subject of this inquiry the people to whom I assign in default of a better name that of Gauda-Dravidian, who by the extensive area they occupied, and over which their descendants are still scattered, are well worthy of a careful research being made into their past history.

PHILOLOGICAL REMARKS.

Before entering upon the historical part of this inquiry, a few general philological remarks will not be out of place. Every one who is even slightly acquainted with the laws which govern the interchange of letters, knows that the labial nasal *m* is often permuted into the other labials as *p*, *b*, or *v* and *vice versâ*. *Mumba* is thus changed to Bombay, and *Mallava* into Ballava; *Marukaccha* is identical with *Bharukaccha*; Sanskrit *pramāṇa* is altered to Kanarese *pavaṇu* or *havaṇu*, measure; *maṭṭai*, stem, in Tamil resembles *paṭṭai*, bark; *madandai* in Tamil, woman, corresponds to *paḍati* in Telugu, and *Maḻḻar* to Paḻḻar, &c. On the other hand, *Bhavāni* becomes Bhamāni; *Vānam*, heaven, is changed in Tamil to *Mānam*; *Palavanēri* to Palamanēri; *Pallava* to Vallama (Velama) and Vallamba; *paḻḻāḍu*, goat, in Tamil, to veḻḻāḍu; *Vaḍavan* to Vaḍaman; the words *Ciṟuvan* and Ciṟuman, *youth*, both occur; *piṟaṅku*, to shine, in Tamil corresponds to the Telugu *meruṅgu*, &c.

The above-mentioned rule is general and applies to other languages as well, for in Greek, *omma*, *e.g.*, becomes *oppa*; *meta*, peda; *membras*, bembras; *pallein*, ballein, and *patein*, batein, &c.; but nowhere else does there exist such a variety and difference of pronunciation as in the vernacular languages of India. Their system of writing is a proof of this fact. Tamil has, *e.g.*, only one sign for the four sounds[1] belonging to each of the five classes; in fact 20 different sounds are expressed by five letters, and even where, as in Telugu, these 20 sounds are provided with 20

---

[1] க் for k, kh, g, gh; ச் for c, ch, j, jh; ட் for ṭ, ṭh, ḍ, ḍh; த் for t, th, d, dh; and ப் for p, ph, b, bh. In their transliteration accordingly are only used *k*, *c*, *ṭ*, *t* and *p*, which indicate the letter, but not the sound.

distinct characters, the pronunciation still remains so uncertain, that in his Telugu Dictionary the late Mr. C. P. Brown arranged these four letters respectively under one head. The cause of this striking peculiarity and these continual permutations is to be found partly no doubt in indefinite pronunciation and dialectical divergencies, but mainly in the strict enforcement of the over-stringent and artificial rules of Sandhi or Euphony, which affect alike vowels and consonants, and which do not, *e.g.*, permit a word in the middle of a sentence to begin with a vowel. Local differences in pronunciation exist in India as well as in other countries. Amongst these the interchanges between *tenues* and *mediae* are most common; we find them in Wales and in German Saxony, where the tenues *p*, *t*, and *k* are to this day confounded with the mediae *b*, *d*, and *g*, or *vice versâ*.

The three Dravidian *l*'s (*l* ல், *ḻ* ள் and *ḻ* ழ்) however differently they may be pronounced, are only varieties of the same sound and are therefore interchangeable, thus, *e.g.*, the Sanskrit *phalam* becomes in Tamil *palam* பலம், or *paḻam* பழம், while *mallam* மல்லம் becomes *maḻḻam* மள்ளம், *veḻḻāḻan* வெள்ளாளன் is also spelt *veḻḻāḻan* வெள்ளாழன், and a village or town is called *palli* பல்லி (*valli* வல்லி), *paḻḻi* பள்ளி, or *pāḻi* பாழி. The harsher sound is generally used by the lower classes, and where these pronounce an ல் *l* or ள் *ḻ*, a high caste-man will lisp a ழ் *ḻ*, which letter is probably a modern innovation prevailing specially in Malayālam and Tamil.

As the different *l*'s interchange between each other, so do the two Dravidian *r* and *ṟ*;[2] a hard double ற்ற் *ṟṟ* is pronounced in Tamil somewhat like a double *ṭṭ*,[3] which circum-

[2] Tamil ர் and ற், Telugu ర and ఱ, Kanarese ರ and ಱ, Malayālam ര and റ.

[3] The Tamil ற்ற் is represented occasionally in Telugu by ట్ల, *e.g.*, the Tamil புற்று, *puṟṟu*, corresponds to the Telugu పుట్ల *puṭṭa*.

stance is a proof of the relationship between the *r* and *ṭ* sounds. After this statement the permutation between the lingual *ḍ* and the *r* and *l* sounds will not create any surprise. Some of these changes are pretty common elsewhere; they occur in the Aryan as well as in the Dravidian languages.

A further peculiarity of the Dravidian languages, and especially of Tamil, is their dislike to beginning words with compound letters: *Brahma* becomes Piramam, பிரமம்; *prabandha*, pirapantam, பிரபந்தம்; *grantha*, kirantam, கிரந்தம். In consequence of indistinct pronunciation and the desire for abbreviation, initial and medial consonants are often dropped at the beginning or in the middle of words, while on the other hand in opposition to this tendency a half-consonant is prefixed to an initial vowel, in order to prevent a word from beginning with a vowel. We thus occasionally meet words whose initial consonants are dropped and replaced by half-consonants, *e.g.*, *vella*, white, in Telugu becomes *ella* and *yella*, *vesa*, haste, *esa* and *yesa*, the name of the *Billavar* of Travancore becomes Ilavar and Yilavar; Vēlūr becomes Ēlūr and Yēlūr. This practice of prefixing a half-consonant before an initial vowel is generally enforced in the middle of a sentence, —a *y* is thus placed before an *a*, *e*, *i*, and *ai* and a *v* before *o*, *u*, and *au*. The half-consonant is used to avoid an hiatus and this explains why the University-degrees M.A. and B.A. are pronounced by many Natives *Yam Ya* and *Be Ya*. Metathesis is likewise of not unfrequent occurrence in the Dravidian languages. It is even found in words of common occurrence, in *kurudai*, *e.g.*, for *kudirai*, horse; in *Marudai* for the town Madura; in *Verul* for Elōra (Vēlūr or Ballōra); in *Vaikāśam* (வைகாசம்) and *Vaikāśi* (வைகாசி) for *Vaiśākham* and *Vaiśākhi*; in the Telugu *agapa* and *abaka*, ladle, &c.

Another peculiarity is to drop one of two consonants in a syllable and to lengthen the vowel if it happens to be short, or to double a consonant and to shorten the vowel, if it happens to be long ; *e.g.*, చెయ్యుట *ceyyuṭa* for చేయుట *cēyuṭa*, *Veḷḷāḷan* for *Vēḷāḷan*, *Palla* for *Pâla*, &c.

It will be readily perceived that this laxity of pronunciation affords a wide field for philological conjectures, and that, if we choose as an example the representative name of the *Malla* or *Palla* tribe, a variety of forms for *Mara* and *Malla*, or *Para* and *Palla*, which actually occur, can be retraced to the common source, and thus be shown to have a sound basis. The task which a philologist has to perform is a serious one and ought to make him cautious. Considerable and unexpected difficulties also arise from the great similarity of many Sanskrit and Dravidian words with *Mara*, *Malla* and their derivatives.[4] The explanations of names of persons, tribes, places, &c., so readily tendered by the Natives

---

[4] A few of such similar words are in *Sanskrit : para*, other, *paḷa*, m., straw, n., flesh, *pala*, m., barn, *pallava*, m., n., sprout, *palvala*, m., pond, *pāla*, m., guard, *pula* great, *phala*, n., fruit, *phāla*, m., n., ploughshare, *phulla*, open, *bala*, n., power, *bali*, m., oblation, *bāla*, young, *bhāla*, n., forehead, *mara*, killing, *mala*, n., dirt, *malli*, f., jasmine, *māra*, killing, *māla*, n., field, *mālā*, f., garland, *valla*, covering, *vallabha*, m., lover, *valli* (ī), f., creeper, &c.; in *Tamil: alam*, plough, *alli*, lily, *alliyam*, village of herdsmen, *aḻai*, cave, *ālam*, water, *palar* (*pallār*), many persons, *palam*, strength, fruit, flesh, *pali*, sacrifice, *pal*, tooth, *pallam*, bear, arrow, *palli*, lizard, *paḻam*, old, *paḻam*, fruit, *paḻi*, blame, *paḷai*, hole, *paḷḷam*, lowness, *paḷḷayam* (*paḷḷaiyam*), offering to demons, *paḷḷaicci*, dwarfish woman, *pāl*, milk, *pālam*, bridge, *pālar*, herdsmen, *pālai*, arid, *pāḻi*, cave, village, *pāḷayam* (*pāḷaiyam*) country, camp, *pāḷi*, encampment, *pāḷai*, palmtree, *pilli*, demon, *pulam*, ricefield, *pulāl*, flesh, *pulai*, flesh, *pul*, meanness, *pullu*, grass, *pullam*, ignorant, *puḷḷi*, lizard, *malam*, excretion, *malar*, flower, *malai*, hill, *mal*, boxing, *mallam*, strength, *malli*, jasmine, *mallu*, wrestling, *maḻai*, rain, *maḷḷam*, strength, *māḷ*, greatness, *mullai*, jasmine, *muḷ*, *muḷḷu*, thorn, *mēl*, above, *valam*, rightside, *valam*, power, *vali*, strength, *valu*, strong, *valai*, net, *vallar*, strong persons, *vallapan*, beloved, *vallavan*, shepherd, *valli*, woman, village, *valliyam*, village of shepherds, *vaḻuti*, poetical epithet of the Pāṇḍya kings, *vaḷappam*, *vaḷamai*, *vaḷam*, *vaḷan*, strength, *vaḷavan*, epithet of Cōḻa, *vaḷḷam*, corn measure, *vaḷḷiyam*, pipe, pepper, *vāḻai*, plantain, *vāḷ*, sword, *vil*, bow, *villi*, Manmatha, *veḷ*, white, *veḷḷam*, inundation, *veḷḷi*, silver, *vēl*, lance, *vēli*, village, *vēḻam*, sugarcane-reed, &c.; in *Telugu : ala*, wave, *ala* (*alla*), then, *alli*, water, lily, *alle*, bowstring, *ela*, young, *ella*, all, limit, white (*vella*), *palla* (*pulla*), red, reddish, *pāḻemu*, camp, *paḷḷemu*, saucer, *pāla*, name of a tree, white, jay, *pālu*, share, milk, *pilla*, child, *pilli*, cat, *puli* (*pulla*), sour, *puli*, tiger, *pulu* (*pullu*), grass, *pulla*, piece, *balla*, bench, *bhāḷi*, affection, *mala*, mountain, *malamu*, dirt, *malu*, again, *malla*

of India and seemingly supported by some legendary and historical evidence, must be viewed with extreme caution and distrust. It is not an uncommon occurrence to make a statement of this kind, and afterwards to invent corroborative evidence. This is often not done with any desire to mislead, but rather because it affords a fair display for speculative ingenuity. If, *e.g.*, a rich man of a high caste acquires a Paṛaicēri, he will alter its name so as to hide the low origin of his property and to impart to it a sacred appearance. Near Madras is situated the well-known hill called St. Thomas' Mount. Its name in Tamil is Paraṅgi Malai or Mountain of the Franks or Europeans, from the original European or rather Portuguese settlement. Some years ago a Brahman settlement was established there and the name of Paraṅgi Malai was no longer deemed respectable. Thenceforth it was changed to Bhṛṅgi Malai, the mountain of the sacred Bhṛṅgi, and eventually in support of this appellation legendary evidence was not slow in forthcoming.[5]

(*malli*) again, *malle* (*mallelu*), jasmine, *māla* (*māle*, *mālika*), garland, *māli*, gardener, *māle*, house, *mulu* (*mullu*), thorn, *mūle*, corner, *mella*, hall, *mēlamu*, fun, *mēlu*, good, upper, *maila*, unclean, *vala*, right, net, *valla*, stratagem, *valle*, noose, *vāli*, custom, *vālu*, long, sword, *vilu* (*villu*), bow, *vīlu*, expedient, *vela*, price, *vella*, white, *velluva*, flood, *vēla*, limit, *vēḷa*, time, *vēlu* 1000, toe, &c.

Considering the changes the letters undergo in Dravidian words, when *paḷḷāḍu*, goat, is also written *veḷḷāḍu* and *pala*, flesh, becomes *pulai* and *Vallūru* is also written *Vālūru*, *Vellūru*, *Yellūru*, &c., similar alterations need not create any great surprise, especially if it is admitted that small orthographical changes assist their being the more easily distinguished. As an illustration how the names of the Mallas and Pallas appear in local appellations I only add as an example a few such names as Mallapur, Pallapur, Ballapur, Vallapur, Yallapur, Allapur, Ellapur, Vellapur, Yellapur, Illapur, Villapur, Vollūru, Ullapur, Vullapur, Malavūr, Palavūr, Balapur, Vālapur, Yālapetta, Ēlapur, Ēlavūr, Vēlapur, Yēlagiri, &c., &c.

[5] An example of the spurious character of similar writings is exhibited by the Sthalapurāṇa that contains the origin of the *Gunnybag-weavers*, which, though of recent origin, is by some incorporated in the Brahmāṇḍa Purāṇa.

A curious instance of the alteration of a name is supplied by the Barber's bridge near St. Thomé in Madras. It was originally named *Hamilton's*

It might appear that when so many changes are possible, no reliance can be placed on such evidence, but these permutations do not all take place at the same time, indeed dialectical pronunciation selects some letters in preference to others. The northern Hindu pronounces, a *B*, where the southern prefers a *V*, and both letters occur only in border districts; thus no *B* is found in the names of such places situated in the Chingleput, South-Arcot, Tanjore, Trichinopoly, Madura, Tinnevelly, and Malabar districts, while in South-Kanara, Ganjam and Mysore a *V* is seldom used.

These few preliminary philological remarks are absolutely necessary to facilitate the understanding of the subsequent discussion. The important position which language occupies in such a research as the present was well pointed out more than forty years ago, by the Pioneer of North-Indian Ethnology, the learned B. H. Hodgson, when he wrote in the preface to his first Essay: "And the more I see of these primitive races the stronger becomes my conviction that there is no medium of investigation yielding such copious and accurate data as their languages."

Historical Remarks.

Turning from these linguistic to historical topics, we know as a fact that when tracing the records of any nation or country as far back as possible, we arrive at a period when all authentic or provable accounts cease. We have then reached the prehistoric stage. What occurred during that epoch can never be verified. When the mist of historic darkness disappears from the plains and mountains of a country, the existing inhabitants and their dwellings become

---

bridge after a gentleman of that name. The word *Hamiltọn*, being difficult to pronounce in Tamil, was changed into *amaṭṭan* (common form for *ampaṭṭan*) which means in Tamil a *barber*, whence by retranslation into English the bridge was called Barber's bridge.

visible, but whether these are in reality the first settlers and their abodes the first erected, is another question which does not properly belong to the domain of history, so long as we are unable to assert its relevancy or to find an answer to it. Whether the people of whom we first hear in a country are really its aborigines may be doubtful; but so long as no earlier inhabitants can be discovered, they must be regarded as such. So far as historical traces can be found in the labyrinth of Indian antiquity, it was the Gauda-Dravidians who lived and tilled the soil and worked the mines in India.

This discussion does not concern the so-called Kolarian tribes, whose connection with the ancient history of India is so very obscure, that we possess hardly any historical accounts about them.

However considerable and apparently irreconcilable may appear the differences exhibited by the various Gauda-Dravidian tribes in their physical structure and colour, in their language, religion, and art, all these differences can be satisfactorily accounted for by the physical peculiarities of the localities they inhabited, by the various occupations they followed, and by the political status which regulated their domestic and social habits. For every one must be aware of the fact that change of abode and change in position have worked, and are working, the most marvellous alterations in the physical and mental constitution of individuals and nations. Language, especially the spirit which pervades it, is the most enduring witness of the connection which exists between nations, and with its help we can often trace the continuity of descent from the same stock in tribes seemingly widely different.

From the north-west across to the north-east, and from both corners to the furthest south, the presence of the Gauda-Dravidian race in India can be proved at a very early period. On the arrival of the Aryans on the north-western frontier, the Gauda-Dravidians are already found in flourishing communities. But successive waves of the Aryan invasion, swelled in their course by the accession of former opponents who had despaired of successful resistance, must soon have flooded over the Gauda-Dravidian settlements. Some by their prowess were able to maintain their ground against the invaders, while others, defeated, left their abodes and emigrated towards the South. Yet even the North, subject though it became in time to the Aryan or rather Brahmanical sway, can never be said to have been totally conquered by force of arms. Still less was this the case with the South, where the Brahmanical influence always assumed a more civic and priestly character; influence, which though of another kind, can hardly be deemed less powerful, since it is more lasting and more thorough. Even the Aryanised languages of North-India—however they may prove the mental superiority of the invaders who were able to force on their defeated foes their peculiar mode of thinking—manifest their origin in their vocabularies and show the inability of the victors to press on the vanquished their own language. The languages of both, victors and vanquished, amalgamated and formed new dialects, and the difference which exists between the abstract synthetic Sanskrit and the concrete agglutinated Dravidian is clearly expressed. This difference is easily observable when we compare on the one hand the construction of Sanskrit with that of such Aryanised languages, as Bengāli and Marāthi, which possess a considerable substratum of a non-Aryan element, and on the other hand the construction of Latin with that of the Neo-latin languages French and Spanish, which may be considered as entirely Aryan. I have alluded to this fact in my "Classification of Languages." Hindustāni is a fair specimen of such a miscegenation of languages.

The earliest mention of a Gauda-Dravidian word is to be found in the Bible. In the first book of Kings, x. 22, we read as follows: *For the king had at sea a navy of Tharshish with the navy of Hiram; once in three years came the navy of Tharshish, bringing gold, and silver, ivory, and apes, and peacocks.*"[6] The expression for peacocks is *tukkiyyīm*, a word derived from the Gauda-Dravidian *toka* (*tokai* or *togai*), which originally signifies the tail of a peacock and eventually a peacock itself. It exists in Telugu, Tamil, Malayālam, Kanarese, Gondi and elsewhere. The identification of *tukki* (*tūki*) with *tokai* is very old indeed, and is already quoted as well known in the early editions of the Hebrew dictionary of Wilhelm Gesenius.[7] The mere fact that the sailors of Solomon and Hiram designated a special Indian article by a Gauda-Dravidian word, renders it probable that the inhabitants with whom they traded were Gauda-Dravidians and that Gauda-Dravidian was the language of the country. The Aryan influence could at that time hardly have been strong enough to supplant the current vernacular, or to force upon it a Prakritised Aryan term. Moreover, the peacock is a well-known bird, common all over India, and it is highly improbable that the Gauda-Dravidians should have waited for the arrival of the Aryans to name it, or should have dropped their own term in order to adopt in its stead an Aryan one. The vocal resemblance between the Hebrew *kōph* and the Sanskrit *kapi* is most likely accidental. The ancient Egyptians, who kept monkeys in their temples, called a monkey *kāf*. Besides it cannot at all be assumed that the sailors of the fleet of Tharshish did not know monkeys. May not *kōph*, *kāf*, *kapi*, &c., after all be an *Onomatopoiëtikon*? Another word which proves the connection of the Gauda-Dravidians with foreign nations is supplied by

[6] The Hebrew words in 1 Kings, x. 22, are: *Oni Tharṣiṣ nōsēth sāhāb vākeseph ṣenhabbīm veqōphīm vethukkiyyīm*. 2 Chronicles, ix. 21, has a long *ū* and reads *vethūkkiyyīm*. The derivation of *ṣenhabbīm* is still doubtful.

[7] See also my lecture *On the Ancient Commerce of India*, p. 25. The derivation of *Almuggīm* or *Algūmmīm* from *valgu* as the sandalwood is called in different places, 1 Kings, x. 11, 12, and 2 Chronicles, ii. 7; ix. 10, 11, is very doubtful, and I hesitate to derive it from Sanskrit.

the Greek word *oryza* for rice, which corresponds to the Gauda-Dravidian *ariśi*, and not to the Sanskrit *vrīhi*.[8]

The Aryan invaders showed little sympathy with the inhabitants they found on the confines and in the interior of India. The outward appearance of the Dāsas or Dasyus—these were the names with which the new-comers honoured their opponents—was not such as to create a favourable impression, and they were in consequence taunted with their black colour and flat noses, which latter made their faces appear as if they had no noses. Indra is invoked to reduce into the darkness of subjection the colour of the Dāsas and to protect the colour of his worshippers, for the latter were not always successful in the combats, and the Dāsas at times turned the tables on their foes by becoming victorious aggressors.

So far as civilisation is concerned, a great difference could hardly have existed between the two races when they first met. However rude may have been the bulk of the indigenous population, a considerable portion of it must have already attained a certain degree of cultivation. It was no doubt the wealth which they had acquired that stimulated the invaders to pursue their conquests, even when a brave

---

[8] See my lecture *On the Ancient Commerce of India*, p. 37 : "Of grains *Rice* formed an important commodity. The cultivation of rice extended in ancient times only as far west as to Bactria, Susiana, and the Euphrates valley. The Greeks most likely obtained their rice from India, as this country alone produced it in sufficient quantity to be able to export it. Moreover the Grecian name for rice *oryza*, for which there exists no Aryan or Sanskrit root, has been previously identified by scholars with the Tamil word *ariśi*, which denotes rice deprived of the husk. This was exactly the state in which rice was exported. The Greeks besides connected rice generally with India. Athenæos quotes *oryza hephthē*, cooked rice, as the food of the Indians, and Aelianus mentions a wine made of rice as an Indian beverage. If now the Greek received their rice from India, and the name they called this grain by is a Dravidian word, we obtain an additional proof of the non-Aryan element represented in the Indian trade."

Arṣi, rice, occurs also in Keikadi, and *ariselu*, ricecakes, in Telugu.

and stubborn resistance warned the Aryans not to drive to despair the various chieftains who had retreated to their mountain strongholds. The bravery of the Dâsas excited the admiration of their opponents. Indra himself occasionally protects the Dāsas, the Aryan priest deigns to accept his offering, and the divine Aśvins partake even of his food. Though both the terms *Dasyu* and *Dāsa* originally denote a destroyer, at times a malevolent superhuman being, and at times in contrast to *Ārya*, an enemy of the gods or a wicked man, and are in this sense specially applied to the aboriginal races who stood outside the Brahmanical pale, yet the expression *Dāsa* continued to be contemptuously used by one Aryan against another, till it became in time equivalent to a common menial or slave.

Division between Gaudians and Dravidians.

The foemen whom the Aryans first encountered were generally brave mountaineers who offered a stout resistance in their numerous castles. Indeed, most tribal names of the inhabitants of India will be shown to refer to mountains.

The two special Gauda-Dravidian terms for mountain are *mala* (*malai*, *pār*, *pāṟăi*, &c.) and *ko* (*koṇḍa*, *kuṟu*, *kunṟu*, *kora*, &c.). Both kinds of expressions are widely used and prevail throughout India. Hence are derived the names of the *Mallas*, *Mālas*, *Mālavas*, *Malayas*,[9] &c., and of the *Kōyis*, *Kōdulu*, *Koṇḍas*, *Goṇḍas*, *Gauḍas*, *Kuruvas*, &c. I shall in future call those tribes whose names are derived from *mala* Dravidians, and those whose names are derived from *ko* Gaudians.

---

[9] Concerning the single and double *l* which is found respectively in Malaya, Malla and in their derivatives, it should be considered that the Dravidian languages do not possess fixed orthographical rules regarding proper names and that single and double letters are often used indifferently. A mountaineer is thus generally described in South-India as *Malayan* or *Malaiyan*, while *Maḻḻan* also denotes an inhabitant of a mountainous district.

PART I.

THE DRAVIDIANS.

CHAPTER II.

THE NAMES OF ANCIENT KINGS AND ASURAS INDICATE THE NAMES OF THE PEOPLE OVER WHOM THEY RULED.

Among the tribes and people whom I regard as Dravidians, whose names are derived either directly from *Mala* or from cognate terms, and who are of the same race as the *Mallas* or *Pallas*, which term is chosen on p. 6 as their representative designation, I may mention the Māras (Mhārs, Mahārs, Mahāras or Mālas), Māris, Maṟavar, Pariahs, Parjas, Paravar, Paravārī, *Πωρούαροι*, Pāratas, *Παροῦται*, Pāradas, Parheyas, Bārs (Bhārs, *Βάῤῥαι*), Brahuis; the Mallas (*Μαλλοί*, Malli), Mālas (Māls or Māras), Mala Arayar, Malacar, Malayālis, Mālavas, (Mālvas), Mālair (Māler or Pahārias), Mallar or Pallar, the Palliyar, Polaiyar, Pulayar, Holiyar, Pulindas (*Πουλῖνδαι*), Puṇḍras, Pallis, Pālas, Pālis, Pallavas (Palhavas, Pahlavas, Pahnavas, Plavas), Pāṇḍyas, Ballas, Bhallas, Bhīls (Bhillas, *Φυλλῖται*), Bhillālas, Ballālas, Vellālar, Velamas (Vallamas, Vallambams), Valluvar, &c.[10]

The Ṛgvēda only rarely confers special names on the Indians who opposed the Aryans, and these names wherever they occur cannot be easily recognised and explained.

On the other hand the Indian gods adopted, particularly in later times, the names of the demons they had defeated in

---

[10] The Māvēlla or *Māvēllaka* whom Lassen in his *Indische Alterthumskunde* (vol. I, p. 751, or 605) identifies with the Megalloi of Megasthenes as occupying Marwar, might perhaps be added to this list.

combat in order to perpetuate the memory of their victories. A natural assumption leads one to infer that the names of the conquered demons or Asuras represent those of the forces they led to battle, and that the Asuras Malla, Bala, Bali, Bāla, Bāli or Vāli, Vala [11] and others were chiefs of the aboriginal race.

Kṛṣṇa is thus called Mallāri,[12] the enemy or destroyer of the Asura *Malla;* Indra is renowned as Valadviṣ or Valanāśana, enemy or destroyer of the demon *Vala,*[13] the brother of Vṛtra, and as Balanāśana and Balārāti, enemy or destroyer of *Bala.*[14] Viṣṇu goes by the name of Balidhvaṁsin,[15] for he defeated the great giant king *Bali* in the shape of a dwarf in the Vāmana Avatāra. Rāma covers his name with doubtful glory by killing in unfair fight the mighty so-called monkey-king *Bāli* or Vāli, the brother of Sugrīva; hence Rāma's name Bālihantṛ.

---

11 Though *Vala* need not be taken in the Ṛgvēda as a demon, he is regarded as such in later works. He may perhaps have been confounded later on with Bala.

12 *Mallāri* or *Malhārī* is in the Maratha country regarded as an incarnation of Śiva, and is also called Khaṇḍōba.

13 Or Valabhit, Valavṛtraghna, Valavṛtrahan, Valasūdana, Valahantṛ, and Valārāti.

14 Or Balaniṣūdana, Balabhit and Balasūdana.

15 Or Balindama, Balibandhana and Balihan. *Bali* or Mahābali was the son of *Virōcana* and father of *Bāṇa*. He ruled over the three worlds, established, according to the Matsya-Purāṇa, at the desire of Brahma, the four castes, and was eventually reduced by Viṣṇu to become the king of Pātāla. He is still the most popular legendary king among the whole Hindu population, especially in South-India. We find a *Mahābalipura* on the *Son* river in the North, and near Madras in the South. The people remember to this day the prosperity enjoyed under his sway. Once a year Bali is said to visit the earth, but this visit is not celebrated simultaneously throughout India. His greatest feast falls on the fullmoon in the month of Karttiki, when the corn standing in the fields, the cow-houses, wells, and particularly the dwelling-houses, are illuminated with lamps. In Mysore popular songs are sung in his praise on the last day of the Navarātri. The Hindu people worship him also during the Pongal, when gourds (in Sanskrit *kūṣmāṇḍa*) are given to Brahmans. Bali is worshipped in Malabar on the Ōṇam festival. He does not die and is one of the seven Cirajīvins.

Beginning of Peaceful Intercourse and Intermarriage between Aryans and Dravidians.

With the decrease of the Aryan immigration into India, their actual conquests ceased and the new comers, once established in the country, devised more peaceful means to perpetuate and extend their power. Colonists and missionaries visited the hitherto unapproached provinces and tried to win by their superior knowledge and civilisation the good will of the natives. Intermarriage recommended itself as the most efficient means to gain this object, though the race-pride of the conquering nation shrank from such misalliances.

In order to sanction them the example of the gods was needed, and Subrahmaṇya, the South-Indian representative of Kārttikēya, the son of Śiva, who delights to reside in wild forests and weird mountain tops is credited with having chosen a South-Indian girl called *Vaḻḻi*[16] as his wife. Vaḻḻi is a well-known female name common among the Pariahs and Paḻḻar, the Paḻḻis and other Śūdras, and corresponds to the equally-widely used man's name Malla. Vaḻḻi is also celebrated as the Amman of Vaiṣṇava gods.[17] The

---

[16] He is the presiding deity of many mountains, as *Tirupparaṅkuṉṟan*, *Cāmimalai* (or Paḻani), *Cōḻaimalai*, &c., and is thus, among other titles, called the ruler of the Paḻani mountain, Paḻani Āṇḍi or Āṇḍavar.

Two wives are generally assigned to Subrahmaṇya. They are called Dēvasēnā (contracted in colloquial Tamil into Tēvānai) and Vaḻḻi. (Vaḻḻi-Dēvasēnāsamēta-Subrahmaṇyasvāminē namaḥ.) Subrahmaṇya is therefore also called in Tamil *Vaḻḻimaṇ(av)āḻan*, or husband of Vaḻḻi.

[17] The popular derivation of Triplicane (Tiruvaḻlikkēṇi) i from *Alli*, அல்லி, a kind of water lily; which explanation I believe to be wrong. According to the Sthalapurāṇa of Triplicane *Nārada* goes to Kailāsa to ascertain from Paramēśvara the position of Bṛndāraṇya which lies north-east of Tiruntrmalai near Pallāvaram. The sage Bhṛgu lived there near a pond full of lotus, called Kairaviṇī. He worshipped the 5 gods of the place, especially Raṅganātha, who slept under a sandal tree. Near it Bhṛgu found a little girl whom he gave to his wife to nurse. He called her *Vēdavalli*, and married her in due time as Vēdavalli Tāyar to Raṅganāthasvāmi, &c. The ancient temple tank in Triplicane is called *Vēdavallipuṣkariṇī*.

principal goddess in Triplicane, who, as Amman presides over the Kṣētram and to whom the temple-compound belongs, is Vēdavalli. The god Pārthasārathi is only lodging there as her guest.[18] In Tiruvallūr the Amman is called Kanakavalli, in Chidambaram Paṅkajavalli, in Srīmusnam Ambujavalli, in Kumbhakōnam there are two, a Kōmalavalli and a Vijayavalli, in Mannārguḍi a Campakavalli, and in Tirumāliruñcōlai as well as in Nāgapatam there is a Sundaravalli, &c. The derivation of Va̤l̤i in these names from the Sanskrit *Valli*, creeper, appears doubtful, especially if one considers that Subrahmaṇya's wife, Va̤l̤i, was a low-caste South-Indian woman, that the Śaiva preceded the Vaiṣṇava creed, and that Śaiva temples were occasionally turned into Vaiṣṇava temples. Pārvatī, the wife of Śiva and daughtor of the mountain Himālaya, is even worshipped as a Pariah woman in her disguise as Mātaṅgī. This word is derived from Mātaṅga, which signifies a wild mountaineer.[19]

---

[18] The difference between *Amman* and *Ammāḷ* (both meaning mothor) is that the former expression refers only to goddesses, while the latter is applied both to goddesses and mortal women.

[19] The Śyāmalādaṇḍaka ascribed to Kālidāsa contains the following ślōka concerning Mataṅgī :—

Maṇikyavīṇam upalālayantīm
  madalasām mañjulavāgvilāsam
Mahēndranilōpalakōmalāṅgīm
  Mātaṅgakaṇyām manasā smarāmi.

It is perhaps not impossible that there exists a connection between *Mātaṅga* and *Mālaṅga*. The *d* and the *l* are occasionally interchanged, compare the Greek δάκρυ with the Latin *lacryma*. The Malayalis consistently pronounce an *l* instead of a *t*, *e.g.*, for *tasmit kāraṇāt* they say *tasmāl kāraṇāl*. In Marathi the word Mātaṅga has been contracted into Māṅga, see p. 66. Compare also the Dravidian roots *paḷa* and *paṇḍu*, old. Telugu has besides *paṇḍu* also *pāta*.

The Amarakōśa, II, Śūdravarga (X) 20, 21, contains the following ślōkas concerning the Mātaṅga and other out-castes.

Caṇḍāla-Plava-Mātaṅga-Divākirti-Janaṅgamāḥ
Niṣāda-Śvapacāv-Antēvāsi-Cāṇḍāla-Pukkasāḥ
Bhēdāḥ Kirāta-Śabara-Pulindā Mlēcchajatayaḥ.

CHAPTER III.

The Mallas.

The name of the Mallas appears in various forms in Sanskrit literature. As the name of a *people*, we meet it in Malaka, Malada, Malaja, Malla, Mallaka, Mallava, Māla, Mālava, Mālavarti, &c.; as the name of a *demon* in Malayaja (Rāhu), Malla (perhaps also if not connected with *mālā*, garland, in Mālyavān and Mālinī), &c.; as the name of a *human being* in Malayakētu, Malayadhvaja, Malayanarapati, Malayaprabha, Malayasiṁha, Malayagandhinī, Malayavāsinī, Mālavī, &c.; as the name of a *country* in Malaya, Malayadēśa, Malayabhūmi, Mallabhūmi, Mallarāṣṭra, Māla, Mālava, Mālavadēśa, Mālavaka, &c.; as the name of a *mountain* or *mountain-range* in Malakūṭa, Malaya, Malayaparvata, Malayabhūbhṛt, Malayācala, Malayādri, Mālyavān, &c.; as the name of a *river* in Mālavī, &c.; as the name of a *town* in Malayapura, Mallapura, Mallavāstu, Mallaprastha, &c.; as the name of a *plant* in Malayaja, Malayadruma, Malayōdbhava (sandal); Mallaja (Vēllaja, black pepper), &c., &c.

If we include in this list some variations of the sound *Malla*, we may mention the three mind-born sons of Brahma, the famous Prajāpatis *Marīci*, *Pulaha*, and *Pulastya*, who had among their progeny the most reputed Daityas or Rākṣasas, as well as the demon *Pulōman*, whom Indra killed, in order to obviate the curse pronounced against him for his having violated Pulōman's daughter *Śacī*. The name *Marīci* occurs also among the Daityas, *Maraka* among the nations, and *mallaja*, black pepper, is likewise called *marica* or *marīca*.

Maru means in Sanskrit a desert and a mountain, and the expression *Marubhū* is specially applied to Mārwār, but its inhabitants as well as the Mhārs are the representatives of an old Dravidian stock, like their namesakes the Maṟavar, மறவர், in South-India. It is in itself very improbable, that these tribes should have obtained their name from a foreign source, and it would not be very venturesome to conjecture without any further authentic proof, that there existed in the ancient Dravidian dialect a word *mar* or *marai* for mountain, corresponding to the synonymous Tamil words *pār* and *pāṟai*. And in fact *mar* in the language of the original inhabitants of Mārwār means *hill*, and the Mārs or Mhārs are in reality *hill men*.[20]

The Mallas, as a nation, are repeatedly mentioned in the Mahābhārata, Harivaṁśa, in various Purāṇas, the Bṛhatsaṁhitā, the Lalitavistara and elsewhere. Mallabhūmi and Mallarāṣṭra, which as well as Malayabhūmi refer to the northern parts of India, occur in the Rāmāyāṇa and Mahābhārata. The Siddhāntakaumudī mentions in a passage that refers to Pāṇini, V. 3, 114, the *Mallāḥ* instead of *Bhallāḥ*, which latter expression is found in the commentary to Dr. O. v. Böhtlingk's edition of Pāṇini. This quotation is significant as the Bṛhatsaṁhitā mentions likewise the Bhallas, who represent the modern Bhillas or Bhīls. Bhalla and Bhilla are identical with Malla and are only different pronunciations or formations of the same word.

The Mallas are specially brought to our notice by the circumstance that Buddha, the great reformer of India, preferred to die among the Mallas in Kuśinagara. The citizens, when they heard of the arrival of the dying saint, met him sorrowfully, and among the last acts of Buddha was that he appointed the Malla Subhadra as an Arhat. This connection of Buddha with the Mallas appears strange and

---

[20] See Lieut.-Col. James Tod's *Annals and Antiquities of Rajasthan;* London, 1829, vol. I, p. 680: The *Mair* or *Mēra* is the mountaineer of Rajpootana, and the country he inhabits is styled *Mairwarra*, or "the region of hills."

strengthens the doubt whether Buddha was an Aryan at all. His name of Śākyamuni and his relationship with the Śākya race has been taken as a reason to associate his name with the Scythian tribes, who had for some time previously been invading north-western India. However this may be, Buddha's friendship with the Mallas supports his non-Aryan origin. The enmity which existed between the kings of Kōśala and the Śākya princes is of itself significant, leaving altogether out of consideration the question whether Buddha was a prince or not. Moreover the inimical position which Buddhism soon assumed towards Brahmanism, the great hold the former took on the non-Brahmanical population, which rushed to be received into its fold, makes the conjecture of Buddha's non-Aryan origin rather probable.

Another branch of the Mallas came into collision with Alexander the Great, while he was progressing towards the South along the valley of the Indus. In the fight which ensued during his attack on their city he was, as is well known, severely wounded. This happened not far from the present Multan, which word I assume to denote Mallasthāna, the place of the Mallas, not Mūlasthāna, as has been assumed hitherto. In fact Sir Alexander Burnes states in his *Travels into Bokhara* (vol. III, p. 114) that "Mooltan is styled 'Malli than,' or 'Mali tharun' the place of the Malli, to this day."

Malayakētu, the son of the mountain king Pārvataka, who figures in the drama Mudrārākṣasa, represents the northern branch of the Mallas, settled in Malayabhūmi, near the Himālaya while the Pāṇḍya kings Malayadhvaja, Malayanarapati, Malayaprabha, Malayasiṁha and others are representatives of the south.

Even to this day the name of the Mallas is preserved among the population all over India, for the Mālas (Māls),

Mala Arayar or Malai Araśar, Malacar,[21] Malayālis, Mālavas (Mālvas), Mālair (Māler or Pahārias), Maḻḻar, Mārs (Māras, Mhārs, Mahārs, Mahāras), Maris, Maṟavar, &c., as they are named in different places, are found scattered all over the country.

The word Malla also shows in its various meanings all the vicissitudes to which individuals and nations are alike exposed. When the bearers of the name were prosperous in the enjoyment of wealth and power, kings were proud to combine the term *Malla* with their own appellation in order to add further splendour to themselves, so that the word *Mallaka* assumed also the meaning of royal, as in the Mṛcchakaṭika;[22] yet when the wheel of fortune turned and the star of the Mallas had sunk beneath the horizon, the former term of honour became degraded into a byname of opprobrium and was applied to the lowest population, so that Mālavāḍu is in modern Telugu the equivalent of Pariah.

Still the recollection of former splendour is not forgotten and is cherished among the Pariahs or Mālas. The Pariahs or Mahārs of the Marātha country claim thus to have once been the rulers of Mahārāṣṭra. And this is not improbable, for not only are the Mahārs found all over the country, but philological evidence is also in their favour. An old tradition divides the Drāviḍa and Gauḍa Brahmans into

---

[21] See Lassen's *Indische Alterthumskunde*, vol. I, pp. 433, 434 (364), note 1: "Die *Malasir* (*Malliars*, *Journal of the R.A.S.*, II, 336) im Waldgebirge Malabars, haben keine Brahmanen oder Guru, verehren als ihren Gott Mallung einen Stein. Auch die Pariar Malabar's haben in ihren Tempeln nur Steine." "Each village (of the Mala Arayar) has its priest, who, when required, calls on the Hill (*Mala*), which means the demon resident there;" see *Native Life in Travancore*, by the Rev. S. Mateer, p. 77. See note 28.

[22] Compare such names as Yuddhamalla, Jagadēkamalla, Trailōkamalla, Ahavamalla, Tribhuvanamalla, &c. See about the *Malla Era*, *Archæological Survey of India*, vol. VIII, p. 203 ff, and about *Mallaka*, Wilson's *Theatre of the Hindus*, vol. I, p. 134.

five classes. The Ślōkas which contain this statement are as follows :—

> Mahārāṣṭrāndhradrāviḍāḥ karṇāṭāścaiva gurjarāḥ
> Drāvidāḥ pañcadhā prōktā Vindhyadakṣinavāsinaḥ.
> Sārasvatāḥ kānyakubjā gauḍōtkalāśca maithilāḥ
> Gauḍāḥ pañcavidhā prōktā Vindhyāduttaravāsinaḥ.

Except the term *Mahārāṣṭra*, all the other names refer to Indian tribes. It may be presumed therefore that this is true likewise in the case of Mahārāṣṭra, and that this name should not be explained by "Great Kingdom." Mahārāṣṭra was also called Mallarāṣṭra, the country of the Mallas. The Mallas are the same as the Māras, who are better known as Mārs or Mhārs. Mhār was eventually transformed into Mahār; in fact both forms exist in modern Marāthi. Two terms identical in meaning *Mallarāṣṭra* and *Mahārāṣṭra*, were thus used. The former dropped into oblivion, and with the waning fortunes of the Mahārs, their connection with the name was soon forgotten and Mahārāṣtra was explained as meaning the "Great Kingdom" instead of the Kingdom of the Mahārs or Mallas. It is indeed curious that the word Pariah has still in Marāthi, the meaning of Mahāra, for the term *Paravārī* corresponds to Pariah, and is used in Marāthi in a general way as a courteous or conciliatory term for a Mahār.[23]

[23] There exist other Ślōkas about this division. The *Skanda-Purāṇa* contains the abovementioned Ślōkas also in the following form :—

> Karṇataścaiva Drāviḍā Gurjarā Rāṣṭravāsinaḥ
> Āndhrāśca Drāviḍaḥ pañca Vindhyadakṣiṇavāsinaḥ.
> Sarasvatāḥ Kanyakubja Gauḍa-Maithilikōtkalāḥ
> Pañca Gauḍā iti khyata Vindhasyōttaravāsinaḥ.

According to Dr. John Wilson: "Maharatta is the Pali form of Mahārashṭra, which with the variant reading Mallarashṭra appears in several of the Purānas. . Now, *Mahārāshṭra* may mean 'the country of the *Mahārs*,' a tribe still known in the province, though in a degraded position, and still so numerous throughout the Marāṭha country that there runs the proverb, *Jenye*

The proper names of *Mallayya* and *Mallaḍu*, common among the Śūdra and Pariah population of Southern India, are occasionally like *Kuppayya* and *Vēmbayya*[24] given among Brahmans and other high-caste people to a boy, when the parents have previously lost two or more children. By this act of humility, displayed in giving a low name to their child, they hope to propitiate the deity and obtain for their offspring the health of a poor man's child. With that object they even throw the infant into a dunghill or *kuppa* (Tamil *kuppai*); a practice which has given rise to the name of Kuppayya.

Step by step the Dravidians receded from Northern India, though they never left it altogether. The Brahmanical supremacy deprived them of their independence, yet not all submitted to Aryan customs and manners. Scattered remains of the Mallas exist, as we have seen, to this day in North-India.

The immense chain of the Vindhya mountains acted as a protecting barrier, otherwise the Dravidians in the south,

---

gānva tenye Mahāra vāḍā. 'Wherever there is a village there is the Mahār ward.' The Mahārs are mentioned by the cognomen which they still bear that of Parwārī (Πωρουαροι) by Ptolemy, in the second century of the Christian era; and in his days they were evidently a people of distinct geographical recognition." See Dr. John Wilson's *Notes on the Constituent Elements.. of the Marāṭhī Language*, p. xxiii in the second edition of the *Dictionary Marāṭhi and English*, compiled by J. T. Molesworth, Bombay, 1857.—Consult too Dr. John Wilson's *Indian Caste*, vol. II, p. 48: "The Mahārs, who form one of its (Mahārāshṭra's) old degraded tribes, and are everywhere found in the province say, that Mahārāshṭra means the country of the Mahārs." Compare *Notes on Castes in the Dekhan*, by W. F. Sinclair, *Indian Antiquary*, vol. II (1874), p. 130. See also Col. Dalton's *Ethnology of Bengal*, p. 264: "We have a tribe called Māl or Mār, scattered over Sirgūja, Palāmau, Belounja, &c."

In the *Vishṇupurāṇa* of H. H. Wilson, edited by Fitzedward Hall, vol. II, p. 165, Mallarāṣṭra is called *Vallirāṣṭra*, and it is conjectured that *Mallarāṣṭra* may be identical with the Mahārāṣṭra (the Mahratta country) of the Purāṇas.

[24] *Vēmbayya* is called after *Vēmbu*, the Margōsa tree, the representative of bitterness. Death should regard in consequence the child as too bitter and too worthless to carry it off.

unlike their brothers in the north, would not have remained so unmolested. In fact the Vindhya mountains were by degrees recognized as constituting the natural frontier between the Aryanised nations of the north and the Dravidians of the south.

Aryan colonisation progressed slowly in the south. The first missionaries appear to have been only visitors and sojourners not permanent settlers in the country, whence they retraced their steps homewards.

The holy Agastya, according to one tradition[25] a grandson of Brahma, a son of Pulastya, a brother of Viśravas and an uncle of the Rākṣasa king, Rāvaṇa, is said to have remained in the South. Many miraculous deeds are ascribed to this diminutive sage. He is said to have been instrumental in the destruction of the powerful Nahuṣa, to have consumed and digested the Rākṣasa Vātāpi, to have drunk the waters of the ocean, and to have forced the Vindhya mountains to prostrate themselves before him. This last feat was intended to symbolize the fact that he having settled down for good in Drāviḍa, became the originator of Brahmanical colonisation. For he exacted from the insurmountable Vindhya, who was lying at his feet, the promise not to rise again until he had returned and recrossed, and as Agastya did not come back, the Vindhya could not lift its head again, and since then the mountain became passable for future immi-

[25] According to another tradition he was born together with *Vasiṣṭha* in a waterjar (therefore called *Kumbhasambhava*, *Kumbhayōni* and *Ghaṭōdbhava*) as the son of Mitra and Varuṇa (therefore *Maitravāruṇi*) and of the Apsaras *Urvaśī*. In the Svāyambhuva Manvantara the name of Agastya, as the son of Pulastya and Prīti, is *Dattōli*. According to the Bhāgavata-Purāṇa Agastya was the son of Pulastya and of Havirbhū and was called in a previous birth *Dahrāgni* or *Jaṭharagni*. (See *Vishṇupur.*, vol. I, p. 154.) He is also called *Pitābdhi* as Ocean-drinker and *Vātāpidviṣ*, as destroyer of Vātāpi. His abode is fixed on the mountain Kuñjara. Many hymns of the Ṛgvēda are ascribed to him. Lassen (vol. II, p. 23) has pointed out the incongruity of the reports respecting the time when he lived, as he is mentioned both as a contemporary of Anantaguṇa and of Kīrtipūṣaṇa Paṇḍya.

grants. Agastya's residence is said to have been the mountain Malayam or Potiyam, not far distant from Cape Comorin ; in the firmament he shines as the star Canopus. To him is ascribed the civilisation of South-India, in fact the most famous ancient Tamil works in nearly every branch of science, such as divinity, astronomy, grammar, and medicine are attributed to him. In consequence he is specially called the Tamil sage (தமிழ் முனி).

EXPLANATION OF THE TERMS DRAVIDA, TAMIL AND ARAVAM.

Sanskrit is called in South-India the northern language or *vaṭa moḻi*, வட மொழி, while the Dravidian goes by the name of the southern language, or *ten moḻi* தென் மொழி. Previous researches have established the fact that the words Draviḍa and Tamil are identical in meaning, that both resemble each other in form, and that Tamil seems to be a derivative from Draviḍa. Yet the origin of the word Draviḍa has hitherto not been explained. Though Draviḍa is generally restricted to denote Tamil: *Draviḍa, Dramiḍa* or *Dramila* is also applied to denote ancient Malayālam; in fact it is properly speaking applicable to all the Dravidian languages. The word Dramila occurs also in Sanskrit literature. I derive Dramila from *Tirumala* and explain it to signify the *sacred Mala* language, as Sanskrit is κατ' ἐξοχήν the refined Aryan language.

It is immaterial to us whether *Tiru* is an original Dravidian word, or a derivation from the Sanskrit *Śrī*, prosperity. Some of the best Tamil scholars of the past as well as of the present day have declared in favour of *tiru* being a pure Dravidian word, and this has all along been my opinion also. *Tiru* was probably in course of time changed to *tira* or *tara*, then contracted to *tra* or *dra*, and finally to *ta* (*da*), both letters *t* and *d* being identical. The Vēda is called in Tamil *Tiruvāy*, the sacred word, and its Tamil adaptation specially used by Vaiṣṇavas is the well-known *Tiruvāy Moḻi.* Tiruvāy was eventually changed to *Taravāy*, which is now generally used in the sense of *Vēda-reading.* The word *Ōttu* does thus in Malayālam signify Vēda and Vēda-reading. The *tiru* of *Tiruvaḻḻaṅkōḍu* has been similarly changed to *tra* in Travancore, both alterations—Draviḍa and Travancore—being no doubt due to the same Aryan influence. From Dramala to Dramila, Damila and Tamil is a short step, unless *Tamil* is directly derived from Tirumala. Dramila, Dramiḍa and Draviḍa are Aryan corruptions of Tirumala and found re-admission into the South-Indian languages as foreign expressions, whose signification was forgotten and defied explanation. I recognize the name Tirumala also in the Tāmala or Dāmala of *Dāmalavarubhayam* near *Pāṇḍamaṅgalam* in the Trichinopoly district. Pāṇḍamaṅgalam is regarded as the old capital of the former kings, among whom the name *Tirumala* did not unfrequently occur. *Ubhayam* (உபயம்) is anything offered or devoted to religious purposes, and *Dāmalavarubhayam* denotes therefore the offering of the Tirumala people, *var* being used as the affix of the Tamil pronoun of the third person plural. *Tirumalarāja* is in colloquial Telugu often called *Tiramalarāyalu*, as *Tirupati* becomes Tirapati. Like *Dāmalavarubhayam* might be mentioned *Dāmalaceruvu* in North-Arcot, *Dāmal* in Chingleput, *Damalapādi* in Tanjore and others. I have been informed on good authority that the last place is to this day also known as Tirumalapādi. Yet, my derivation of Tirumala does not require the support of the etymology of these names.

Another but rarer form of Dramila is *Drimila*, which is derived from *Tirumila*, as Tripati from *Tirupati*, Trikōvil for *Tirukōvil*, or Trikāl for *Tirukāl.* The fact of the term *Tamil* being the ultimate derivative from Tirumala (Tramala) and denoting a special Dravidian dialect will perhaps serve in future researches as an historical clue for fixing the period when the various vernaculars of Southern India became separate and distinct languages. If the *Limyrikē* (Λιμυρική) of Ptolemy (VII, 1, 8 and 85) is the *Dimirica* repeatedly mentioned in the Cosmography of the anonymous geographer of Ravenna, as Bishop Caldwell has clearly pointed out by identifying it with Damirice or the Tamil country (see p. 14 of the Introduction to the second edition of the *Comparative Dravidian Grammar*), the work of Ptolemy contains the earliest mention of the word *Tamil.*

All these permutations prove the continual interchange of *m* with the other labial consonants, and of *l* into the *d* and *r* sounds.[26]

---

[26] With respect to the above-mentioned conjectures a few observations are perhaps necessary.

The change of *a* into *i* and *vice versâ* is not rare, as in *mala* and *mila*, *Damirica* and *Dimirica*, *tiṟa*, open, and *taṟa*, &c., &c. *Tiruvāy* and its slang alteration into *Taravāy* are both Tamil words, though the latter common form has been introduced into Telugu by Telugu Brahmans—especially by Vaiṣṇava Telugu Brahmans—who live in the Tamil country, and has thus found its way even into modern Telugu dictionaries. The term *Taravay* for Vēdādhyāyana or Vēdōpakrama is neither found in Kanarese and Malayalam, nor in pure Telugu. The most important lesson which Brahman boys have to learn at and after their *Upanayanam* or investiture with the holy thread are Vēda mantras. Children generally alter words so as to suit their pronunciation, and Tamil boys most probably invented *Taravāy* for *Tiruvāy* as they say *taṟa*, open, instead of *tiṟa*. This corrupted form found eventually access into common Tamil, for up to this moment Taravāy is only considered a slang term. The origin of the word once forgotten, *tara* of *taravāy*, was connected with the word *taram* in the meaning of *time* (once, twice, &c.), and as every lesson in order to be known must be repeated, so also the reciting of the Vēda after so many times or *taram*. It seems to be overlooked by those, who prefer this explanation, that the term *Taravāy* is only applied to the repetition of the Vēda and not to any other repetition, that if *tara* had been taken in the sense of "*time*," it ought to be at the end of the word, and that the syllable *vāy* gives no sense in *taravāy* unless it is accepted as meaning *Vēda* or holy word. *Taravāy*, *taruvāy*, in *taravāta* and *taruvāta*, occur in Telugu in the meaning of *afterwards*, as do in Kanarese *taravāya* and *taruvāya*; but these words have nothing in common with the above-mentioned Tamil *Taravāy*. The elision of an *r* is also not unfrequent, as *trāguṭa*, to drink, in Telugu becomes generally *tāguṭa*. Already Bishop Caldwell was struck with the strange formation of the word Dravida, for he says: "The compound *dr* is quite un-Dravidian. It would be *tira* in Tamil; but even if we suppose some such word as Tiraviḍa or Tiramiḍa to have been converted into Dravida by the Sanskrit-speaking people, we get no nearer to

The Telugu, Kanarese and other cognate northern races, when they had forgotten their claim to the name of Dravidians, called the Tamil language *Aravam*. This word *Aravam* is most likely a corruption of Draviḍam. Draviḍam or Dramilam became in its turn Daramiḍam (Daramilam), Araviḍam (Aravilam), and finally Aravam.[27] However peculiar these changes may appear to the uninitiated, to the scientific philologist they can afford no special difficulty. Even in Sanskrit we occasionally observe an initial *d* dropped, *e.g.*, in *aśru*, tear, which is δάκρυ in Greek, *thräne* in German, and *lacryma* in Latin; while the elision of

---

an explanation of the original meaning of the word." See Introduction to *Comparative Dravidian Grammar*, p. 13.

The name *Tirumala* becomes in colloquial Telugu also *Tiramala*, *Tirmala* and *Timma*. This last word must be distinguished from *Timma* for *timmaḍu* or *timmanna*, monkey. Similarly does *tāmbūlamu*, betel, become tamalamu (or tammalamu) and *tāmma*; and *tāmara*, lotus, *tammi*.

In Tamil the verb *ōtu* (ஓது) means to recite the Vēda, while *ōttu* (ஓத்து) signifies the Vēda itself. Both words are Tadbhavams formed from the Sanskrit word *Vēda*.

[27] The Tamil form *Tiraviḍam* for *Draviḍam* appears to prove that the origin of the word *Draviḍa* had been forgotten, when it was re-introduced into Tamil. As the Telugu and Kanarese languages do not insert an *i* between two consonants in the same manner as Tamil does, the derivation of *Aravam* from *Draviḍam* gains in probability. In Kanarese the Tamil people are besides called *Tigaḷar*, which I am inclined to consider also as a corruption for Trimala. The *r* in the first syllable was dropped, and the labial in the second has been changed into a guttural *g*, as is not unfrequent; compare, *e.g.*, Kuḍaman and Kuḍavan with Kuḍagan. *Tigala* and *Arava* have in this case the same meaning. I am aware that the Rev. Mr. Kittel, whose opinion carries much weight, has declared that the original form of *Tigaḷar* (*Tiguḷar*) was *Tigur̤ar*.

The derivations of *Aravam* hitherto proposed appear to me to be inappropriate. Dr. Gundert thought it could be connected with *aṟam*, virtue, and *aṟavan* would have the meaning of a moralist. Others preferred the Tamil word *aṟivu*, knowledge, and *aṟivan* or *aṟavan* represented thus the Tamulian as the intelligent person of the South, others derived it from an obscure Tamil district *Aruvā*. The defect of these etymologies is the fact that the Tamil people ignore the word *aravam*, so far as their name is concerned. The Telugu pandits are in favor of *arava* meaning *a-rava*, without sound, for the Tamil language does not possess aspirates, or is according to others rather rough; while some Kanarese pandits proposed as its root the Kanarese word *aravu*, half, or deficient, as the ancient Kanarese people are said to have

medial consonants is not at all unusual in the Indian vernaculars, *Bēstāramu*, Thursday, in Telugu, *e.g.*, for Bṛhaspativāra, *jannidamu* for yajñōpavīta, *ānati* for ājñapti.

The importance I attach to the derivation of Dravidian from Tirumala in the specified sense can be duly appreciated only when one considers that it establishes at once the prominent position the Malas (Mallas) or Dravidians occupied in the whole of India. It may perhaps be interesting to quote from the eloquent preface of Hodgson on the Kocch, Bōdo, and Dhimāl Tribes the following sentences, in which the term Tamulian is employed as equivalent to Dravidian. "The "Tamulian race, confined to India and never distinguished "by mental culture, offers, it must be confessed, a far less "gorgeous subject for inquiry than the Arian. But, as the "moral and physical condition of many of these scattered "members of the Tamulian body is still nearly as little "known as is the assumed pristine entirety and unity "of that body, it is clear that this subject had two parts, "each of which may be easily shown to be of high "interest, not merely to the philosopher but to the states-"man. The Tamulians are now, for the most part, British "subjects: they are counted by millions, extending from "the snows to the Cape (Comorin); and, lastly, they are as "much superior to the Arian Hindus in freedom from dis-"qualifying prejudices as they are inferior to them in know-"ledge and all its train of appliances. Let then the student "of the progress of society, of the fate and fortunes of the "human race, instead of poring over a mere sketch of the past,

---

regarded Tamil to be a deficient language. Bishop Caldwell has treated at some length on this subject in his Introduction, pp. 18-20.

The initial consonant is often dropped in Dravidian languages, *e.g.*, in Tamil *Avai*, assembly, for *cavai; alliyam*, village of herdsmen, for *valliyam; aḷai*, rat hole, for *vaḷai* and *paḷai; amar*, war, from Sanskrit *samara; alam*, plough, from Sanskrit *hala; ita*, agreeable, from Sanskrit *hita;* in Telugu *esa*, haste, for *vesa; ella*, white, for *vella; ēyuṭa*, to throw, for *vēyuṭa; ēnu*, I, for *nēnu; īvu*, thou, for *nīvu; ēmu*, we, for *mēmu*, &c., &c.

"address himself to the task of preparing full and faithful "portraits of what is before his eyes; and let the statesman "profit by the labours of the student; for these primitive races "are the ancient inheritors of the whole soil, from all the rich "and open parts of which they were wrongfully expelled."

As points of minor interest I may as well here mention that the words Tirumāl and Perumāl are also derived from Mala (Malla). Both terms were originally the titles given by the Mallas to their great chiefs and kings. Each Perumāl was at first elected to rule for a period of twelve years, and was chosen from outside the country to govern Malanāḍu or Malayāḷam. As it often happens elsewhere with royal names, these were in later times applied as honorific appellations to the specially revered god, in this instance to Viṣṇu. The terms *sacred Mala* or the *Great Mala* being once connected with the deity, lost their original meaning, which was in course of time entirely forgotten. This circumstance explains their peculiar derivations so often found in Tamil dictionaries, and the strange attempts of grammarians to explain their startling formations. The name of Perumāl, the great Mala, is still a royal title in Malabar.[28]

CHAPTER IV.

The Pariah (Pārata, Pahāria), Brahui, Bār (Bhār), Mār (Mhār), &c.

Before I turn to the Mallas known as Pallas, I shall, after a few remarks, discuss the position of the Pariahs

---

[28] The *māl* in Tirumāl is generally derived from *māl*, illusion, while the same *māl* in Perumāl is explained as a change for *mān* in the synonymous *Perumān*. The word Tirumāl supplies the best evidence of the radical nature of the *l* in Perumal.

The indigenous title of the South-Indian Cēra, Cōḷa and Pāṇḍya king was *Perumāl*. *Mallan* was the name of a Perumāl who built Mallūr in

and kindred races. The *Paḻḻar* are described in Dr. Winslow's Tamil and English Dictionary as "a low dependent caste employed in husbandry, &c., under their feudal lords, a peasant tribe dwelling in the south, supposed to be a change of Maḻḻar, மள்ளர்." Though the Paḻḻar, like the Paḻḻis and other tribes regard themselves as the descendants of the Pallavas once so powerful, they themselves neither produce nor possess sufficiently reliable historical evidence in support of their claims, which nevertheless may be perfectly well-founded. I have often but in vain tried to obtain some authentic information from the various castes in corroboration of their assertions, but I have only received vague and unreliable statements.

Derivation of the word Pariah.

If the term *Pariah* is considered to signify every outcaste from every caste, then the Pariahs, as such, do not come within the scope of this discussion; for though the greater part of them belong no doubt to the original or rather aboriginal Dravidian population, from which they have in later times been severed by hereditary social rules, and though they in their turn acknowledge among themselves caste distinctions, yet as every outcaste becomes to a certain extent a Pariah, the term Pariah does not represent now a strictly ethnological sub-division.

On the other hand it must be admitted that irrespective of this foreign element which has been added to the Pariah community, the Pariahs represent a distinctly separate class of the population, and as such we have to deal with them here. The general name by which the Marātha Pariahs is known is *Paṛavārī*.

Pōlanāḍu. *Mallan* is also called a rural deity which is set up on the border or on the ridges of rice-fields. Compare Dr. Gundert's *Malayālam Dictionary*, p. 801, and note 21 on p. 21.

That their name, in spite of its usual derivation from *paṟa* or *paṟai*, drum, should rather be connected with the name of the original Dravidian population, seems to me to admit of no question. The supposition that the Pariahs are the drummer-caste and have obtained their name from that instrument appears to rest on a weak foundation. It is most probably an afterthought, the more easily explicable since the lower classes delighted in the noise of the drum, and the name of the drum-beating class was transferred to the instrument by which the Pariah made his presence known. The lute of the Caṇḍāla (the *caṇḍāla-vallakī*, *caṇḍālikā*, *cāṇḍālikā*, *kaṇḍōlī* or *kaṇḍōla-vīṇā*) is similarly named after the Caṇḍāla, and not the Caṇḍāla after the lute. Moreover, the word *paṟa* or *paṟai* is, except in Malayālam and Tamil, not found in the other Dravidian languages in the sense of drum and at the same time as the name of the Pariahs; for the Pariah is called *Holeya* in Kanarese in spite of *paṟe* signifying a drum, and in Telugu he is known as *Mālavāḍu*, which word originally signifies *mountaineer* (see pp. 21 and 56). If the Pariahs were really the caste of drummers, they would most probably be called so, wherever they are found in India.

I regard the Pariah as the representative of the ancient Dravidian population, and as having been condemned to supply his name to the lowest layers of the population, as the ancient Śūdras after their subjugation gave their name to the Śūdra caste. It will be subsequently shown that the *Caṇḍālas* are among the Gauḍians, what the *Pariahs* are among the Dravidians. This connection is even indicated by the name of the Caṇḍālas, which resembles those of the Kandaloi, Khands and Goṇds.

I think that the word *Pariah*, the *Paravārī* of the Marātha country, is intimately connected with the names of the Pāratas, Pāradas, Paravar, Pardhis, Parheyas, Pahārias or Māler, Bārs (Bhārs), Brahuis, Mārs (Mhārs), &c., &c., and that it designated originally a *mountaineer*, from the Dravidian root *paṟa*, preserved in the Malayālam *paṟa*, in the Tamil *pār* and *pāṟai*, and the Telugu *pāru*. The formation of the word *Pahāria* corresponds probably with that of *Mahāra*, and as Mahāra or Mahār is derived from Mhār and Mār, as *Bahar* is from Bhār and Bār, so may also *Pahār* be regarded as a derivative from Phār and Pār.[29]

---

[29] Bishop Caldwell remarks on p. 549 on this subject: "It has been said "that the name Pareiya, or Pariah, is synonymous with that of the Paharias "(from *pāhār*, a hill), a race of mountaineers, properly called Mâlers, "inhabiting the Rājmahal Hills, in Bengal; and hence it is argued that the "Pareiyas may be considered, like the Paharias, as a race of non-Aryan, non-"Dravidian aborigines. It is an error, however, to suppose that there is "any connection between those two names. The word Pariah, properly "Paṟeiya, denotes not a mountaineer, but a drummer, a word regularly "derived from *paṟei*, a drum, especially the great drum used at funerals. "The name Pareiya is, in fact, the name of a hereditary occupation, the "Pareiyas being the class of people who are generally employed at festivals, "and especially at funerals, as drummers."

The improbability of this derivation, though advocated by such a great authority as the highly esteemed and learned Bishop, has been pointed out by me. Moreover, it may be remarked that Pariah drummers are not employed at the festivals of Brahmans.

As the name of the Pariah is thus by high authorities derived from *paṟai*, drum, it is here perhaps not out of place to mention some of the various kinds of drums used by the natives of Southern India. The drums vary as to their size, construction, the material they are made of, and the manner in which they are carried. A *Ḍamāra* (Sanskrit *Ḍamaru*) is carried by a bull, a *Ḍhaṅka* (Sanskrit *Ḍhakkā*) on a horse, a *Nagārā* (of Semitic origin, in Arabic, *e.g.*, نقارة; Tamil *Nakarā*) by an elephant or camel, and a *Bhēri* (Sanskrit *Bhēri* (ई)) on a cart. Other kinds of drums are carried by men, as the *Tappaṭṭai*, a small drum, which hangs from the left shoulder and is beaten under the left arm from below with a stick in the right hand, and from above with a small stick in the left hand. The *Tāsā*, a small semi-globular shaped drum, is worn in front round the neck below the chest and beaten with two small sticks. The *Ḍōl* (Sanskrit *Ḍhōla*) is a big drum which is also carried over the neck, but is beaten only with one stick in the right hand and with the other hand. The *Paṟai*, which has the euphemistic name of *Alaṅkāram*, is not carried, when beaten, but lies on the ground between the feet of the drummer and is used at festivals, weddings, and funerals. It is beaten only by a particular class of Pariah the *Veṭṭiyān*, who burns corpses and digs graves. It is therefore neither beaten by all Pariahs nor used in common life. The *Tappaṭṭai* and *Tāsā* are in fashion among the Pariahs and other low classes, though Muhammedans and Śūdras practise on them occasionally. The beaters of the other drums are mostly Śūdras. The *Kōtas* and the *Todas* on the Nilagiri also have the *Tappaṭṭai* and Tāsā. The term *paṟai* is in Tamil now used as the general term for drum. I believe that most of the

5

THE BRAHUIS.

On the northern frontier of India near the Bolan Pass not far from the seats of the ancient Bhalānas, who are mentioned by the bards of the Ṛg-vēda, begins the long chain of the *Brahui* mountains. This mountain range extends continuously from the vicinity of the Bolan pass to Cape Monze on the Persian Gulf, and is to this day the home of the Dravidian Brahuis, who must be regarded as the western borderers of Dravidian India. The origin

---

above-mentioned names of the drums are merely imitations of the sounds these instruments make. H. H. Wilson introduced by mistake the "*Palaya* or *Paraya*" in his translation of the second edict of Aśōka. The *Mālalu* or Telugu Pariahs are also called *Mannepuvāṇḍlu* or Highlanders; see *Ind. Antiq.*, vol. VIII, p. 218.

Compare Fr. Buchanan's *History, Antiquities, Topography and Statistics of Eastern India*, edited by Montgomery Martin, vol. II, pp. 122, 123: "The mountain tribes are, I believe, the descendants of the original inhabitants of the country, very little, if at all, mixed with foreign colonies. Their features and complexion resemble those of all the rude tribes, that I have seen on the hills from the Ganges to Malabar, that is on the Vindhya mountains. Their noses are seldom arched and are rather thick at the points.. Their faces are oval..Their lips are full..Their eyes..are exactly like those of Europeans." See Lassen, *Indische Alterthumskunde*, vol. I, pp. 454-458 (1st ed., pp. 380-384): "Die Pahāria nennen sich selbst Maler oder Bergbewohner,..sie haben dieselben Züge und die Hautfarbe, wie alle die rohen Stämme vom Ganges nach Malabar . . es soll die Sprache der Pahāria reich an Worten sein, die dem Tamil and Telinga zugleich angehören." On p. 1028 Lassen remarks in note 5: "Est is zu bemerken, dass *Pārada* zwar auch Bergbewohner bedeutet haben wird."—I believe that the *Parjas* of Jeypore should be included among these people, though Mr. D. F. Carmichael prefers to regard this name as a corruption by metathesis from the Sanskrit word *Prajas*, subjects. See *Manual of the District of Vizagapatam*, p. 87; Madras Census Report of 1871, vol. I, pp. 223–225.—One of the *Koli* tribes on the Mahi Kanta hills is called *Pariah*. Two Rājput tribes of Mallāni are known by the name of *Paria* and *Pariāria*.

The fishermen in Tinnevelly are called *Paravar* (or *Paratar* and *Paratavar*). According to Mr. Simon Casie Chetty in his "Remarks on the Origin and History of the Parawas" in vol. IV of the *Journal of the Royal Asiatic Society*, pp. 130-134: "It is the general belief among the Parawas that their "original country was Ayudhya, or Oude; and it appears that previously to "the war of the Mahābhārat, they inhabited the territory bordering on "the river Yamuna, or Jumna... In that section of the Mahābhārat entitled "*Adipurva*, it is said, that the king of the Parawas who resided on the banks "of the Jumna, having found an infant girl in the belly of a fish adopted "her as his own daughter, giving her the name of *Machchakīndī*, and that

of the names of the Baluches [30] and of the Brahuis is unknown, but I believe that they are in some way related to, if not indeed identical with, each other. I recognise in the name of the Pāratas [31] and Pāradas who dwelt in North-eastern Baluchistan,—which country coincides with the Paradēnē of Ptolemy,[32]—the origin of the modern word Brahui. Both the Sanskrit as well as the Dravidian languages possess the two liquids *r* and *l*, yet the former letter seems to have

---

"when she grew up, she was employed (as was customary with the females "of the Parawa tribe) to ferry passengers over the river. On a certain day, "the sage *Parāsara* having chanced to meet her at the ferry, she became "with child by him, and was subsequently delivered of a son, the famous "Vyâsa, who composed the Purânas. Her great personal charms afterwards "induced king *Santanu*, of the lunar race, to admit her to his royal bed, and "by him she became the mother of *Vachitravirya*, the grandsire of the "*Pândavas* and *Kauravas*.. Hence the Parawas boast of being allied to the "lunar race, and call themselves accordingly, besides displaying at their "wedding feasts the banners and emblems peculiar to it."

This is the story of *Satyavatī* (*Matsyagandhī*), the mother of Vyâsa by Parâśara, and of Vicitravīrya and Citrāngada by Śantanu, which is told in the *Ādiparva* in the 63rd and 100th chapters and elsewhere, as also in the Harivaṁśa, XVIII, 38–45. Compare also J. Talboys Wheeler's *History of India*, vol. I, pp. 60–62.

It is peculiar that the *Pallevāṇḍlu* in the Telugu country who correspond to the Pallis in the South are mostly fishermen, though the same term *pallevāṇḍlu* applies also to *villagers*. In North India a class of fishermen is called *Malla*. The name denotes the tribe and not the occupation.

[30] The modern Baluches say that they came from Aleppo in Syria. Little is known about the origin of their name. It resembles that of the Ballas and Bhalânas, though it is unsafe to make any conjecture in this respect.

[31] See Bṛhatsaṁhitâ, x, 5, 7; xiii, 9; xiv, 21, &c. Varâhamihira mentions the Pâratas together with the Râmaṭas, and with other nations on the northern frontier of India, *e.g.*, Śaka-Yavana-Darada-Pârata-Kâmbōjaḥ. The Pâradas occur in Manu (x. 44), in the Ramâyaṇa, and repeatedly in the Mahâbhârata, Harivaṁśa and Viṣṇupurâṇa.

It has been also proposed to explain *Pârada* as meaning a people living across the river, in this case beyond the Indus. Such a name could hardly have been assumed by the *Pâradas* themselves, especially if they had never crossed the Indus.

[32] When describing Gedrosia Ptolemy VI, 21, 4, says: Τὰ μὲν οὖν ἐπὶ θαλάσσῃ τῆς χώρας κατέχουσιν Ἰρβιτῶν κῶμαι, τὰ δὲ παρὰ τὴν Καρμανίαν Παρσίδαι (ἢ Παρσίραι), τὰ δὲ παρὰ τὴν Ἀραχωσίαν Μουσαρναῖοι, ἡ δὲ μέση τῆς χώρας πᾶσα καλεῖται Παραδηνή, καὶ ὑπ' αὐτὴν Παρισιηνή, μεθ' ἣν τὰ πρὸς τῷ Ἰνδῷ κατέχουσι Ῥάμναι. Besides *Paradēnē* may be mentioned as connected by

been preferred in more ancient times, as is seen, in the Vedic words *aram*, enough, and *rarāṭa*, forehead, instead of the later *alam* and *lalāṭa*. The same peculiarity has been observed in ancient Iranian, and no valid objection can be raised against connecting the word *Parthva* of the cuneiform inscriptions (the classical *Parthiva*) with Pahlav. The Parthians were Scythians or Turanians and so were the Pallas (Mallas) of India and their neighbours on the northern frontier of India.

The power of the Parthians becoming supreme in Persia, the name became identified with Persia, and after the disappearance of the Parthian or Pahlavi kings the words *Pahlavi* assumed in course of time the meaning of *ancient Persian* and even of *ancient*. It is a curious coincidence that in the Dravidian languages also a word resembling *Palla* in form means *old*, in Tamil and Malayālam *paḻa*, in Kanarese *paḻe* or *haḻe*, in Tulu *para*, etc. Under these circumstances I regard the *Bra* in Brahui as a contraction of *Bara*, and obtain thus in *Barahui* a name whose resemblance to that of the ancient *Barrhai* the modern Bhārs, as well as to that of

---

similarity of name and vicinity of geographical position the districts *Parsia*, *Parsiana* and *Parsiene*, the tribes of the *Parnoi* (Arsaces and Tiradates are said to have been Parnians), *Parūtai*, *Parsidai* or *Parsirai* and *Parsyētai* and the mountain range of the *Paropamisos*.

According to the command of the king Sagara, the *Yavanas* shaved their heads entirely, the *Śakas* shaved the upper half of their heads, the *Pāradas* wore their hair long, and the *Pahlavas* let their beards grow. (See Harivaṁśa, XIV. 15–17).

Sagaraḥ svām pratijñām ca gurōr vākyam niśamya ca
dharmam jaghāna tēṣām vai vēśānyatvam cakāra ha. 15
Arddham Śakānām śirasō muṇḍayitvā vyasarjayat
Yavanānām śiraḥ sarvam Kāmbōjānām tathaiva ca, 16
Pāradā muktaklēśāśca Pahlavāḥ śmaśrudhāriṇaḥ
nissvādhaya vaṣaṭkārāḥ kṛtāḥ tēna mahātmanā. 17

Compare also *Vishṇu Purāṇa* of H. H. Wilson, edited by F. Hall, vol. III, p. 294.

Bishop Caldwell mentions that the practice of wearing long hair is characteristic of the Dravidians. (See *Dravidian Grammar*, 2nd edit., Introduction, p. 114.) Beards are also worn by many Dravidian races.

the Pāratas and Paravar, and their kindred the Marātha *Paravāri* and Dravidian Parheyas of Pālamau is striking. It is also not impossible that the country Paraśa, which corresponds to Northern Baluchistan and not to Persia, and is mentioned in Hiven-Tsiang's travels, contains the same name. The interchange of *r* and *l* is equally apparent in the name of the Māras or Mālas of Pālamau, who derive their origin from Mālva. The connecting link between the Brahuis and the ancient Dravidians through the Bhārs, Parheyas, Mārs and Mālas, &c., seems to be thus established.[33]

The Bārs or Bhārs.

After the Brahuis the aboriginal Indian race of the Bārs or Bhārs claims our attention. The earliest mention of them is found in Ptolemy VII, 2, 20, where they are called

---

[33] The late Dr. Trumpp was fully persuaded of the Dravidian character of the Brahui language. With respect to the explanation of the name most authorities seem to admit that the first syllable *Bra* is originally dissyllabic. The *Journal of the Royal Asiatic Society* contains in vol. XIX, pp. 59–135 "An Essay on the Brahūi Grammar" after the German of the late Dr. Trumpp, of Munich University, by Dr. Theodore Duka, M.R.A.S., Surgeon-Major, Bengal Army. On p. 64 we read: "The national name, "Bráhûi is pronounced in several ways. Nicolson and Maulawi Alla Bux "spell it Biruhi (that is Bíroohi or Birouhi), but we must not forget that "Birúhí (बिरूही) is a Sindhi word, and it is therefore difficult to say how "the people in question call themselves. In Nicolson's Reader the word "occurs twice written براهوى, which cannot be pronounced otherwise than "Bráhúí or Birāhúi, and this should, therefore, be adopted as the proper "pronunciation of the word."

This statement is not quite correct; it can as well be pronounced *Barahui*, for برا, large, is pronounced *barā*, and برابر, abreast, *barābar*, &c.

According to Mr. C. Masson *Brahui* is a corruption of Ba-roh-i.

The word Brahui appears to indicate a *highlander*, for a tribe of the Baluchis is called *Nhārui*, not a hill man, *i.e.*, a dweller in the plain. The Nhāruis "may be considered to hold the same place with reference to the Brahuis that 'lowlanders' do to 'highlanders'." See *The Country of Balochistan*, by A. W. Hughes, p. 29.

My derivation appears thus to have a good foundation.

See Dr. Fr. Buchanan's *Eastern India*, edited by M. Martin, vol. II, p. 126: "The northern tribe consider their southern neighbours as brethren, and call them Maler, the name which they give themselves; but the southern tribe, shocked at the impurity of the others, deny this consanguinity, and

Barrhai. They do not appear to be specially quoted in Sanskrit literature, unless the wild mountaineer tribe of the *Bharatas*, who occur in the dictionaries along with the *Śabaras*, is considered identical with them. Sir Henry M. Elliot thought that the Bhārs might perhaps be the Bharatas, whose descent is traced to Jayadhvaja. According to the Harivaṁśa the Bharatas are very numerous. The Bhārs pronounce their name very harshly, and it is by no means impossible that the well-known Aryan word barbarian, *Barbara* or *Varvara* in Sanskrit, owes to a certain extent its origin to them.[34] The Bhār tribe is also known as *Rājbhār*, *Bharat* and *Bhārpatva.*[35] There is some contention between the Bhār and the Rājbhār as to superiority, but this is a difficult point to decide; some regard the Rājbhārs as

---

most usually call the northern tribe Chet, while they assume to themselves the denomination of Mal or Mar, which however is probably a word of the same derivation with Maler." Compare also note 23 on p. 22, and *Descriptive Ethnology of Bengal*, by Colonel E. T. Dalton, p. 264 : "We have a tribe called Māl or Mār..They declare, they came originally from Malwā. ..Malwā is the chief seat of the Bhīl race, who are considered aborigines of that district. Mālavas and Bhils may be identical, and our Pahārias and Bhīls cognates."

[34] See Genl. Sir A. Cunningham in his *Archæological Survey of India*, vol. XVII, p. 140 : "We know at least that the Aryans ridiculed the aborigines on account of their *burr*, and gave them the nick name of *barbaras*, or barbarians, from which we may conclude that any words containing the burred *r* must be indigenous."

The word *barbar* is spelt in Hindustāni *baṛbaṛ*, بڑبڑ. Compare "Notes on the Bhars and other Early Inhabitants of Bundelkhand," by Vincent A. Smith in the *Journal of the Asiatic Society of Bengal* [1877], vol. XLVI, pp. 227-236, where in the first note on p. 227 we read : "The name is usually spelt 'Bhar,' but the spelling 'Bharr' would more accurately represent the pronunciation."

[35] See Sir Henry M. Elliot's *Supplemental Glossary of Indian Terms*, vol. I, pp. 33 and 34 : "Common tradition assigns to them the.. whole tract from Gorakhpūr to Bundelkhand and Saugor, and the large Pargannah of Bhadoí, in Benares (formerly Bhardaí) is called after their name. Many old stone forts, embankments, and subterraneous caverns in Gorakhpūr, Azimgarh, Jaunpūr, Mirzapūr, and Allahabad, which are ascribed to them, would seem to indicate no inconsiderable advance in civilization. The wild Bhīls of Marwar are called Bhaunrīs, but I know not whether there is any connexion between them and the Bhars. The Bhoyas and Bhuttias of Agorī and

descended from the old Bhār nobility, who themselves claim to have been formerly Kṣatriyas. They do not eat swine's flesh as the Bhārs do, and this abstention is regarded as an indication of greater respectability. All these races are now very much mixed. The Bhārs are often mentioned together with the Cherus.

We possess very little information about the ancient history of the Bhārs. Legend associates their name with the earliest Aryan heroes, *e.g.*, with *Rāma* and his sons, but the Bhārs suddenly disappear from the scene, and, so far as history is concerned, reappear just previously to the Mahommedan invasion of India, at which period they certainly possessed a vast territory, and were indeed the real owners of the soil.

In fact the Bhārs must have once ruled over a great area of country stretching from Oudh in the west to Behar in the east and Chota Nagpur, Bundelkund and Sagar in the south. Their name still survives in Bahar, Bahraich (Bharaich), Bāra, Baragaon, Bāra Banki, Barhapara and Barwan in Oudh, in Bareilly, Barhaj, Barhar (or Bharhar) in the North-Western Provinces, in Bar, Barabar, Baraghi and Barhiya in Behar, in Barva in Chota Nagpur, and in many other places.[36] *Bāra* in Oudh is said to have been founded

---

Singraulī, who are generally classed as Ahīrs, may probably bear some relation to the Bhars, though no trace can now be had of their descent. Tho Cherūs also are sometimes said to be a branch of the Bhars. . . It is strange that no trace of Bhars is to be found in the Puranas, unless we may consider that there is an obscure indication of them in the 'Brahma Purana,' where it is said that among the descendants of Jayadhvaja are the Bharatas, who, it is added, 'are not commonly specified *from their great number*,' or they may, perhaps, bo the Bhargas, of the Mahabharata, subdued by Bhim Sen on his Eastern expedition. The Bhars consider themselves superior to Rājbhars, notwithstanding the prenomen of Rāj, but this claim to superiority is not conceded by the Rajbhars. They do not eat or drink with each other."

See *Harivaṁśa* XXXIII, 53 : Bharatāścā sutā jātā bahutvānnānukīrttitāḥ.

[36] See *The Bhars of Audh and Banáras*, by Patrick Carnegy, Commissioner of Rāi Barelī, Oudh, printed in the *Bengal Asiatic Journal*, vol. 45, p. 303 : " The parganas of Bhardoi, Bharosā, Bahrāich, and Bharolī and the

by a Bhār Rāja called Bāra, while the foundation of *Bāra Banki* is associated with Jas, another Bhār Rāja. The Liṅga on the top of the *Bārabār* hill near Gayā was according to local tradition placed there by a Bār Rāja, whose combats with Kṛṣṇa are even now remembered by the people.[37] This is most probably an allusion to the Asura *Bāṇa*, the son of Bali. The *Bārhapāra* pargana is still populated with aboriginal Bhārs. The pargana *Bhādohi* or *Bhārdohi* is called after them, and the name of the town of *Bharaich* is also derived from their name.[38]

Traces of the former supremacy of the Bhārs are found scattered all over the country. Most of the stone erections, fortifications, as well as the embankments, and the subterranean caves in Gorakhpur, Azimgarh, Janpur, Benares, Mirzapur, and Allahabad are ascribed to them. Such forts generally go now by the name of *Bhār-dīh*. The grand ruins known as those of Pampāpurā in the neighbourhood of the modern

town of Bhartipur (near the Bhar capital, Kusbhawanpur *alias* Sulṭānpūr), are all believed to derive their names from the Bhars.. Sleeman also mentions a large district of nearly a thousand villages near Mahamdi, which even in his day was known as Bharwāṛā, now occupied by Ahban Rajpūts." Compare *Bengal Asiatic Journal*, vol. 46, pp. 227 and 228 : "The former presence of the Bhars in the Hamīrpur District is attested by the traditions, which will be presently described, and by local names in every pargana. A few examples of such names out of many may be of interest; thus the old name of the town of Sumerpur (in Parg. Sumerpur) is Bharuā, and in the parganas of Maudhā, Panwārī-Jaitpur, Jalālpur, and Raṭh, respectively, we find localities named Bharsawān, Bharwārā, Bharkharī or Barkharī, and Bhaṇṛaurā Kerā, and in several of these cases the evidence of the name is confirmed by that of tradition." With respect to *Baragaon* Genl. Sir A. Cunningham (*Archæological Survey of India*, vol. I, p. 28) says: "By the Brahmans these ruins (of Baragaon) are said to be the ruins of Kundilpur ..I doubt the truth of this Brahmanical tradition, more especially as I can show beyond all doubt that the remains at Baragaon are the ruins of Nâlanda, the most famous seat of Buddhist learning in all India."

[37] About *Barabar* compare *Arch. Survey of India*, vol. I, pp. 40-53. Sir A. Cunningham derives the name from "*bara* and *awara*, or *Barawara*, the great enclosure (see p. 43)," as there was an enclosure on the Siddheśvara hill. See *ibidem*, vol. VIII, pp. 35-37.

[38] Genl. Sir A. Cunningham identifies the *Bardaotis* of Ptolemy with Bharhut. See *Arch. Survey of India*, IX, pp. 2-4 and XXI, p. 92. Compare also *Bengal Asiatic Journal*, vol. XVI, pp. 401-416.

Mirzapur probably owed their origin to the Bhārs. Mr. C. A. Elliot states that "almost every town whose name does not "end in *pūr*, or *ābād*, or *mow*, or is not distinctly derivable "from a proper name, is claimed by tradition, in the east of "Oudh, as a Bhar town. The district of Bharaich . . . is their "oldest abode, and the name of the town Bharaich is said "to be derived from them." Traces of the Bhārs abound according to Mr. Duthoit, late Superintendent of the Maharaja of Benares, "on all sides in the form of old tanks and village forts. One cannot go for three miles in any direction without coming upon some of the latter." Not very long ago the Bhārs were the lords of the soil in the districts of Benares and Oudh, and according to the still prevailing tradition in Azimgarh, the Rājbhārs occupied the country in the time of Rāma. The structures left by the Bhārs prove that they were equally proficient in the arts of peace and of war. The remains ascribed to them are especially numerous in the Benares district.[39]

Benares or Vārānasī (Bārānasī) lies on the banks of the *Barna* (or *Varaṇā*), where it flows into the Ganges. I am of opinion that *Bārānasī* owes its name to the Bārs or Bhārs. I assign likewise the name of *Behar* or Bahar to the same origin, especially as the Bhārs were once the rulers in this district, and as the usual derivation from *Vihāra*, a Buddhist temple, seems to me very problematic, the more so

---

[39] Compare Sherring's *Hindu Tribes and Castes*, vol. I, pp. 357-375 on the Bhar tribe, and the *Archæological Survey of India*, vol. XII, p. 89: "It is said that Nagar Khās and Pokhra, and the land generally around "the Chando Tāl, were originally in the possession of the Bhars, who may "possibly, therefore, have founded some of the ancient sites in that "neighbourhood." Read also *Bengal Asiatic Journal*, vol. XLV, p. 305, about the *Bharādīs* (or Bhar-ābādīs).

On the other hand, Mr. Smith, *ididem*, vol. XLVI, p. 234, remarks: "The Bhars of Bundelkhand, so far as we know them, seem to have "possessed little of the arts of civilization, and to have consequently left "behind them almost nothing of architectural or artistic interest."

6

as Behar was not the only district in India which was covered with such religious buildings. Not far north from the old town of Behar lies to this day the district and village of *Bar*. *Bahar* is also the name of a small place in Oudh. It might perhaps be advisable to discontinue deriving the names of Indian localities from Sanskrit words, as has been usually done hitherto, unless where such derivations are well supported. General Sir A. Cunningham thinks that too much stress has been laid upon the popular traditions which ascribe nearly all the ancient remains to the Bhārs.[40] But, impossible though it may be to prove the authenticity of the legends, it can hardly be doubted that a good deal of truth does underlie them.

In the explanation of the local names a great difficulty arises because many words of Sanskrit, Persian, Arabic and

---

[40] See Gen. Sir A. Cunningham, *Archæological Survey of India*, vol. XI, p. 67: "It has been the fashion to refer all the remains of antiquity in Eastern Oudh to the barbarous race of aboriginal Bhars."

Instead of proving the incorrectness of such statements, that may be, and indeed are, wrong in some cases, Sir Alex. Cunningham substitutes another etymology, to which also many *real* objections can be made. He is in favor of substituting for the name of the *Bhar* people that of the baṛ (banian) tree, which is in Sanskrit *Vaṭa*. Speaking of the native *burr* as mentioned on p. 38, in note 34, he continues on p. 140 of vol. XVII: "To "this class I would refer the name of the banian tree, *bat*, which is "invariably pronounced *bar* or *war*, with a burring *r*. Hence, as *da* means "water in several of the aboriginal dialects, we have *Wardā*, or the 'Banian "tree river.' That this is the true derivation of the name seems nearly "certain from the plentifulness of the banian tree in the Warda district, "where we also find the names of *War-ora*, *Warar*, *Wargaon*, *Warhona*, "*Warha*, *Wargai*, *Warjhari*, *Warkuli*, *Warnera*, and *Waḍnera*, and *Baḍnera*, "several times repeated; and even the name of Berār itself is said to be "properly *Waṛ Hār* or *Baṛhār*, the country of the *baṛ*, 'a banian tree.'"

Some of these etymologies appear very doubtful, especially those of *Wargaon* and *Berar*. I should perhaps remark that the places given by Sir Alex. Cunningham differ from those quoted by me on p. 39. It is also peculiar that most of the localities above mentioned are written with an initial *W*. Compare also the notices about the Banian (*Bar*) forests in the *Haveli* pargana in the *Archæological Survey of India*, vol. XVIII, pp. 52–54, and vol. XXII, pp. 13–15.

other origin are very similar to the tribal name of the Bhārs.[41]

These people formed no doubt a considerable portion of the old population of Northern India. Though the Aryan power was for some time paramount in this part of Bharatavarṣa, and our historical accounts about the Bhārs begin at a considerably later period—in fact after the Buddhist reformation—we are as yet unable to define the time of the supremacy of the Bhārs. I am of opinion that the Aryan invaders subdued the Bhārs, and kept them in the background till they in their turn were vanquished by other intruders. The non-Aryan population continued to occupy the ground as previously in the capacity of landowners, farmers and serfs. The Buddhist re-action brought them again to the front. Some of them who were landholders or farmers were called Bhūmiyas, from *Bhūmi*, land, and are now known by this name.[42]

---

[41] E.g., *bār*, *bhār*, *bhārā*, burden; *bār*, signifies also in Hindustāni according to the various words from which it is derived, time, water, prohibition, &c.; *bārā*, boy, *bārah*, twelve, *bar*, excellent, *barr*, wasp, *barā* and *baṛā*, large, *baṛ*, Indian figtree, &c.

[42] See General Sir A. Cunningham in the *Archæological Survey of India*, vol. XI, pp. 130-131: "There is a ruined fort on the hill above the village "(Bhuili). The derivation of the name is not known, but I suspect it to be "connected with the great tribe of *Bhuïas*, and that it may be only a "slightly altered form of *Bhuïāla*. The Bhuïas are by far the most numer-"ous class in the Chunār and Sahsarām districts. They are evidently the "aborigines or old inhabitants of the country. Buchanan writes the name "Bhungihar, but I believe that the proper appellation is simply *Bhūmia*, or "men of the earth, or *autochthones*, a title given to them by the Brahmans. "They generally call themselves *Musahar*."

See the *History*, *Antiquities*, *Topography and Statistics of Eastern India*, edited by Montgomery Martin; London, 1883, vol. I, p. 168: "The "Bhar have been fully mentioned in my account of Puraniya, in the north-"western parts of which, and in the adjacent parts of Tirahut and Nepal "they were at one time the governing tribe;" further, pp. 176, 177, 178: "In this district the most numerous of these tribes is called *Musahar*, and they, "probably like the *Bhungiyas*, are the remains of the armies of Jarasandha. "In some parts, Musahars and Bhungihars are reckoned two names for "the same tribe, which is probably a just opinion (176). The *Rajwars* are a

As many changed or disowned their tribal name, the seeming disappearance of the Bhārs can be explained to a great extent. They were also largely absorbed by other

---

"pretty numerous tribe (177). They pretend that their common ancestor was "a certain Rishi, who had two sons. From the eldest are descended the "Rajwars, who became soldiers and obtained their noble title; from the "younger are descended the Musahars, who have obtained their name from "eating rats which the Rajwars reject... They differ in scarcely any of their "customs from the Musahars....The *Rajwar* and *Bhungiyas* are allowed to be "higher than the Musahars....They all speak a very impure dialect of the "Hindi..The Musahars live chiefly in little round huts, like bee-hives; "but the huts of the Bhungiyas and Rajwars are of the usual form. The "Bhungiyas and Rajwars have chief men called Majhis, like those of the "hill tribes in Bhagalpur." (178); vol. II, p. 119.

About the Musahar read: "The Mushcras of Central and Upper India," by John C. Nesfield, in the *Calcutta Review* of January 1888, pp. 1–53. On p. 2, Mr. Nesfield says: "In Buchanan's *Eastern India* they are "described as a people 'who have derived their name from eating rats.' "In an old folk-tale, which has recently come to my knowledge, the name "is made to signify flesh-seeker or hunter (being derived fron *masu*, flesh, "and *hēra*, seeker)."

Compare Dalton, *Ethnology of Bengal*, pp. 81, 82, 92, 130, 148—

"The *Kocchis* then gave a line of princes to Kamrup; at this time a part "of Upper Asam was under a mysterious dynasty, called the Bhara Bhuya, "of which no one has ever been able to make anything (81) ..All the works "still existing in the deserted forests of the northern bank of the Brahma-"putra are attributed to the Bhara Bhungyas or Bhuyas (82). (Buchanan, "vol. II, p. 612, mentions already the legend of the 12 persons of *Bārah* "*Bhuiyas*.)..The *Kocch* appear to me equally out of their element among the "Lohitic tribes.. In short I consider they belong to the *Dravidian* stock, and "are probably a branch of the great Bhuiya family, and we thus obtain a clue "to the tradition of the Bhara Bhuiyas, to whose period of rule so many great "works in Asam are ascribed (92).

According to Colonel Dalton, p. 327, the Rājwārs in Sirgūja "are skilled "in a dance called *Chailo*, which I believe to be of Dravidian origin."" See the two articles "On the Barah Bhūyas of Eastern Bengal," by Dr. James Wise, in the *Bengal Asiatic Journal*, vol. LXIII, pp. 197–214, and vol. LXIV, pp. 181–83. Dr. Wise relates the history of five Bhūyas, *i.e.*, of Fazl Ghāzī of Bhowāl, Chand Rāi and Kedar Rāi of Bikrampūr, Lakhan Mānik of Bhaluah, Kandarpa Nārāyana Rāi of Chandradīp, and Īsā Khān, Masnad-i-Ali of Khizrpūr.

Compare further *Note on Mahāsthān near Bagurā (Bogra), Eastern Bengal*, by C. J. O'Donnell, *ibidem*, LXIV, pp. 183–186. On page 183 we read: "With regard to Mahasthan he (the District Deputy Collector) seems more "correct. He identifies it with *Bārendra*, the capital of the Bārendra "Hindus. In favour of this view the only arguments are strong, though

castes and communities, but a sufficient number of them still exists.[43]

Many Rājputs have Bhār blood in their veins, and Dr. Francis Buchanan went so far as to state that the *Parihāra* Rajputs of Shahabad are descended from the Bhārs.[44]

"simple. The whole country between the Ganges, the Mahānandā, Kāmrūp, "and the Karatoyā, was undoubtedly the old Barendra Desha. To the "present day, much of it is called 'Barind.'.. All round it, however, there "are shrines, holy wells and embankments connected with the name of "Bhīma, one of the Pāṇḍava brothers .. Bhīma is said to have made a large "fortified town south of Mahāsthān, which is marked by great earthworks "altogether about eight miles long, and still in places as much as twenty "feet high. The whole country between them and Mahāsthān is in places "covered with bricks... It may be mentioned in connection with Mahasthān "that there is a legend that on a certain occasion twelve persons of very "high distinction and mostly named Pāla came from the west, to perform "a religious ceremony on the Karatoyā river, but arriving too late, settled "down on its banks till the next occurrence of the holy season, the Nārāyaṇī, "which depends on certain conjunctions of the planets, and was then twelve "years distant. They are said to have built numerous places and temples, "dug tanks, and performed other pious acts. They are said to have been "of the Bhuinhār or Bhāman Zamindār tribe, which is, at the present day, "represented by the Rājās of Banāras and Bhettia." See also *Archæological Survey of India*, vol. XV, p. 115.

[43] The Census of 1881 counts 382,779 Bhars, of whom 20,870 live in Bengal, 1,639 in the Central Provinces, and 360,270 in the North-Western Provinces.

[44] See Dr. Buchanan's report in Montgomery Martin's vol. II, p. 463: "In the account of Shahabad I have mentioned, that those pretending to be such (*Parihar Rajputs*) were in fact *Bhars* or Bhawars, and the same might be supposed to be the case here (in Gorukhpoor), where the Bhars were once lords of the country; but the Bhars here do not pretend to have any kindred with the Parihars, and the latter are not only allowed to be a pure but a high tribe;" and vol. I, 493: "The tribe of palanquin-bearers, including *Parihar Rajputs*, *Rajbangsi Bhars*, and *Rajbars* amounts to about 500 families."

Compare P. Carnegy in the *Bengal Asiatic Journal*, vol. XLV, p. 300–2. "Many years of the official life of the writer have been devoted to duties "which involved the examination of the genealogies of some of our oldest "and best native families, and the results of his inquiries have led him to "the following conclusions: (1) that not a single member of the landed "gentry or local priesthood can trace back to an ancestor who held an acre "of land, or who administered a spiritual function within the area under "inquiry during the Bhar supremacy; (2) that scarcely any of them can "trace back to an ancestor who came into Audh at the Muhammadan advent,

The Bhārs like other tribes have embraced the different creeds, which from time immemorial prevailed in India;

"when the Bhars, who were then in universal possession of the land, were "overthrown; and (3) that the great mass of the landowners of to-day can "trace no further back than to an ancestor whose origin is easily discovered "to be both indigenous and spurious... I have found the opinion so gener- "ally entertained that there was a Rajpūt conquest and colonization of "Audh, that it requires a distinct answer...I have not discovered the exist- "ence of any such central tradition of conquest by Rājpūts from without.. "I can refer to the histories of many Rajpūt clans,..but none of them declare "..the arrival of an army of clansmen, and colonization by the victors with "their families and kin. The very fact of the singular connections to which "so many of the clans trace their descent is opposed to the idea of a con- "quest by arms. An orthodox Hindu, the conqueror of a low-born race, "would not have founded a family by an alliance which his religion sternly "rebuked...It is finally noticeable that the Audh clans who claim an extra- "provincial origin, trace their descent to single Chatrīs, and not to troops "of Rājpūt invaders. Such are the Bais of Baiswaṛa,..and the Rajkumārs. "..With these two exceptions none of the clansmen of eastern Audh claim a "western origin. In regard to the *third* class, it is always invidious to "enter into details of *pedigrees*, but a few amongst very many available "instances may be given. The Kanpūriā is one of our most important "clans; so is the Bandelgot. In twenty generations according to the "members, both these pedigrees are lost in obscurity; but what the world "says is this, that they are the offspring of mal-alliances between two "Brahman brothers, and women of the Ahīr and Dharkar tribe. The "Amethia is not an unimportant clan. They call themselves Chamār-gor "Rājpūts, and their generations are not longer than the other named. "What the world says of this, is that a Chamār-gor is the offspring of a "Chamār father and a Gor-Brahman woman. Moreover within the memory "of man, an Amethia Chief has, according to Sleeman, taken to wife the "grand-daughter of an ex-Pāsī Chowkildar and raised up orthodox seed "unto himself. The Raotars are another numerous clan with but half the "number of generations, and with precisely a similar parentage as the Kan- "pūriās (Brahman-Ahīr). Their name is taken from Rawat, an Ahīr chief. "The Pulwars are influential and numerous, and of these it is said that they "are descended from a common ancestor, who had four wives, of whom "one only was of his own status, the others being a *Bharin*, an *Ahīrin*, and "another low caste woman. Here we have a Hindu-Bhar origin freely "admitted. The Bhalesaltan clan, also, is comparatively modern, and of "equivocal Ahīr origin. There are numerous families of Bais, too, who are "in no way related to the Tilokchandī Bais of Baiswaṛā. The former are "modern and equivocal, the term Bais being, it may be mentioned, the most "ready gate by which enlistment into the fraternity of Rājpūts could for- "merly be achieved.... Finally, all those landowning families, who can only "urge an indigenous origin, must, whether they admit it or not, recognise "the fact that they are descendants of Bhars, for every acre of land was

but Buddhism and Jainism were naturally more popular than any other foreign religion.[45]

A considerable number of Bhārs fills the post of village policemen, while others are ploughmen, but the vast majority of this race are now in a miserable condition.

In spite of the abilities they exhibit when suitably employed, and in spite of the reputation of their ancestors which has survived to this day, the descendants of the ancient rulers of the land have now lost nearly everything and are reduced to the most abject condition.

The Mārs, Mhārs, Mahārs, Mhairs or Mers.

While speaking about the Mallas I availed myself, on pp. 21 and 22, of the opportunity of introducing the Mahārs or Mhārs, whom I recognised as the people who had given their name to *Mahārāṣṭra.* But it was not to that country alone that the Mahārs were confined, for they have always been occupants of Rājputāna. The provinces which now go by the name of (Ajmere) Mhairwāra and (Jodhpur) Mārwār are their ancient home. "The *Mair* or *Mera* is," according to Colonel Tod, "the mountaineer of Rajpootana, and the country he "inhabits is styled *Mairwarra* or the region of hills." These hillmen by and bye populated the plain and are also found there.[46] They remained masters of the soil until they were ousted later on by victorious invaders. As chiefs and warriors, like other aboriginal tribes, they have a claim to be

"owned, and the country was throughout peopled by these alone and by "no others."—Compare also the article "On the Bhar Kings of Eastern Oudh," by W. C. Benett, in the *Indian Antiquary*, vol. I, 1872, pp. 265 and 266.

[45] Compare *Bengal Asiatic Journal*, vol. XLV, p. 303.

[46] See *Annals and Antiquities of Rajasthan* by Lieutenant-Colonel James Tod, vol. I, 680.—The name of *Mārwār* is generally connected with Sanskrit *maru*, desert, mountain, rock. I believe this derivation to be wrong, though it gives a pretty good explanation of the diversified nature of the country, which is hilly in one part and arid in the other.

called Rājputs, for the name of Rājput or Rājaputra confers only a social, and not an ethnological distinction. The term Rājput is generally applied to an Aryan Kṣatriya, though everybody knows that the victors intermarried freely with the vanquished non-Aryans, who were never totally annihilated, and that the Mārs and other non-Aryan tribes claim relationship with the Rājputs.

No real ethnological difference between a Mār (Mhār, Mahār) and a Mhair (Mer) has been found to exist. It has been previously mentioned that, according to Colonel Dalton, "Mār or Māla is a very uncertain name applied "to or assumed by different people in different parts of India, "but it may be that there is some affinity between all the "tribes who bear it."[47]

Many Mārs (Mhārs) have clung to their hills as strongholds; some have comfortably settled down as cultivators, while by far the greater part are exposed in consequence of their indigence to severe oppression, and are treated like Pariahs. In fact, the history of the Mār (Mhār) resembles that of the Bhār and the Pariah, and, like the latter, he has also retained in the Dekhan a small amount of influence. For, according to Mr. R. N. Gooddine, "he is the "watchman and guardian of the village and the living chro-"nicle of its concerns. His situation or his curiosity makes "him acquainted with everybody's affairs, and his evidence "is required in every dispute. Should two cultivators quarrel "respecting the boundaries of their fields, the Mhār's evidence "ought to decide it, and should a similar quarrel happen "between two villages, the Mhārs are always the chief actors

[47] See Tod's *Rajasthan*, vol. I, 681; Hunter's *Imperial Gazetteer of India*, vol. I, 97: "All the inhabitants of Mhairwara bear the common title of Mairs or hillmen, which, however, must be regarded rather as a geographical than as a social or religious distinction:" and VII, 514, "Most of these (the Minas and Mhairs) claim irregular descent by half-blood from Rajputs, while some of them are closely connected with the Bhils."

"in it, and to their decision alone it is sometimes referred. "The Mhār is emphatically called the *village-eye*."[48]

The Maṟavar.

The *Maṟavar* in Madura and Tinnevelly likewise claim the position of Rājputs, and if we regard them as a warrior tribe, they are entitled to this distinction. They are also most probably in some way connected with the Mārs of the north. The Maṟavar have to a great extent preserved their freedom and independence. They are brave, warlike, and self-willed like most semi-barbarous races, but they have latterly taken to more peaceful pursuits than they used to follow formerly. They were once very numerous, but are now greatly reduced in numbers. Their chief is the *Sētupati* of *Ramnād*, one of the oldest and most respected princes in Southern India, and who is still highly honored by,

---

48 See this extract from Mr. R. N. Gooddine's Report on the "Village Communities of the Dekhan," in vol. II, pp. 207-208 of Rev. M. A. Sherring's *Hindu Tribes and Castes*, as well as Sherring's further remarks.

Mr. W. F. Sinclair says (see *Indian Antiquary*, vol. III, 1874, pp. 130, 131): "The *Mahārs* or *Dheḍs* are the most important caste of Parwaris. Whether they are the aborigines of the country or not, there does not seem to be any way of deciding; but it seems to me that the term Mahārāshṭra, generally translated 'country of the Marāṭhās,' is at least as likely to mean 'country of the Mahars;' and I throw this out for more learned Sanskṛitists to decide upon. However, they are a very important people in it now, nor must it be supposed that their position, though socially low, is without its rights and dignities . . . The Mahār, as I have mentioned, is not only the guardian of boundaries, but also of the public peace and health, as watchman and scavenger; of communications, for he should guide travellers and make petty road repairs; and of the public treasure and correspondence, for it is his duty to carry the revenue to the treasury, and convey all messages on account of Government. It will be seen that he has no sinecure (and) . . it is obvious that he is not one 'of the Queen's bad bargains.' These duties belong to the Mahār as *yeskar*, or village watchman . . . But the *Tarāl* or gate-ward, an officer found in a good many villages, is generally also a Mahār by caste. The term *Dheḍ* is simply Hindustanī for a Mahār and is found as we go northward." Compare "Two Lectures on the Aboriginal Race of India," by Lieut.-General Briggs, *Royal Asiatic Soc. Journal*, XIII, pp. 275-309, specially p. 281. See my remarks about the origin of the term *Mahārāṣṭra* on pp. 22 and 23.

and exacts honors from, the surrounding chiefs and princes. The active life which the Maṟavan leads in the open air has imparted to him great bodily strength. He can be easily distinguished from other natives by his good figure and generally erect and proud bearing.[49]

The Pariah, Pahāria, Parheya, the Brahui, Bār or Bhār and the Mār, Mhār or Mahār of our day should, as I hope to have proved, be regarded as the descendants of the original Dravidian population. I am of opinion that all these tribes, whose names contain the letter *r*, are the representatives of the first and oldest stratum of the Dravidian race, and that the descendants of the *Malla* or *Palla* are those of the second stage, from which the other part of the present Dravidian population has been gradually evolved.

Religious and Social Privileges enjoyed by Pariahs.

In Mysore the *Holiya* or *Holeya* (ಹೊಲಿಯ, ಹೊಲೆಯ takes the place of the Pariah. The word Holiya may be another form for Pulaiya, unless we assume that the *l* in Holiya is a change from *r* and connect the word Holiya with Paṟaiya.

However despised a position the Pariah and the Holiya occupy in the places where they live, they have preserved and still cherish, as the Mhār and Bhār do, the memory of former greatness and regard themselves as the original owners of the soil. Political revolutions, about which we now know nothing, have most probably been the cause of

---

[49] Maṟavan also means originally *mountaineer*, but Mr. Nelson in his *Manual of Madura*, has quoted (II, p. 39) a legend, according to which the Maravar sided with Rama against Ravaṇa, and Rama thanked them and "exclaimed in good Tamil, *Maravēn* or 'I will never forget'; and that they "have ever since been called Maravans. With more probability the name "may be connected with the word *maram*, மறம், which means killing, "ferocity, bravery and the like." See Nelson's *Manual*, II, p. 38–42, on the Maṟavar.

their subversion by other kindred Dravidian tribes. Yet, considering the unstable nature of the Indian states, the continual disturbances and fighting which give to Indian history such an unpleasant and unsatisfactory appearance, there seems nothing peculiar in the claims advanced by those Pariahs, who are in reality the descendants of the original inhabitants. The Pariah calls himself to this day the elder brother of the Brahman, claiming in this manner precedence of the Brahman. The Brahmans on the other hand ascribe the origin of the Pariahs, Caṇḍālas, and other low castes to the connection of Brahman women with low caste men, or to the curse which sages, like Viśvāmitra, were so fond of uttering against their own flesh and blood, or against any one who was unfortunate enough to come across them at an inauspicious moment. The legend of the curse of Viśvāmitra's sons is interesting, as it ascribes to them the origin of some wild tribes like the Āndhras, Puṇḍras, Śabaras, and Pulindas.[50]

The Pariahs have according to the *Ñānaveṭṭi* eighteen titles like the Veḷḷāḷar and possess also the same insignia.[51]

The chief goddess of the Pariahs is called *Āttāḷ* or *Ammāḷ*, mother, and represents Pārvatī as mother of the earth, while

---

[50] The elder fifty of the hundred sons of *Viśvāmitra* offended their father, and being cursed by him, became outcastes and the forefathers of all the wild tribes.

According to an old tradition, found in the Purāṇas and retold in the *Kulasaṅkaramālā* of Veṅkaṭācalācāryar of Rāyapuram and in the Kanarese *Sōmēśvaraśataka*, Vasiṣṭha was the son of Urvaśī, the famous divine prostitute, and the husband of a Caṇḍāla woman of the Cakkili caste, who was in reality *Arundhati*, reborn as a Caṇḍālī. As such she bore him one hundred sons, ninety-six of whom disobeyed their father and reverted to the Pañcama (fifth) or Pariah caste, while the four others remained Brahmans.—*Agastya* was, as already intimated on p. 24, n. 25, in this birth the brother of Vasiṣṭha.

[51] Among these insignia are mentioned the following: white, earth-circle umbrellas; lion, swan, green and white, monkey (*Hanuman*), cuckoo, plough-handle, wheel and lion faced flags; a trumpet; closely carried torches (*aruku*) and day torches; victorious bells, two white chowries, white elephant; white horse; ivory palanquins; cuscus fan, flute; white petticoat, two poles with cloth across the street (*makaratōraṇa*), golden pot, &c.

as *Piḍari* she resembles through her evil inclinations Kālī. Different personifications of Pārvatī and Kālī are variously named, as Vēḷāttāḷ (Ēḷāttāḷ), Nāgāttāḷ, Ēgāttāḷ, Cēmāttāḷ, Māriyāttāḷ or Mariyamman, Aṅgāḷamman, Ellamman, Puṅganamman (Puṅgāttāḷ), &c. Temples are found everywhere in South India, and she is generally the village goddess. *Māriyamman*, the goddess who inflicts and removes small-pox and other diseases, is found among the Gauda-Dravidians of the whole of India.

The feasts of these goddesses extend over a week and last occasionally sixteen days. During the whole of this time a Pariah is kept clothed and fed in the temple as the accepted bridegroom of the goddess. High across the streets festoons of margosa leaves are hung, and on the last day, while pots filled with water are carried by the people and the idol is taken in procession round the streets of the village, tom-toms are beaten in honor of the Pariah bridegroom, and after he has fasted and bathed, he gets a new cloth dyed with saffron, and the priest fastens a quarter anna piece to the right hand of the goddess and another to that of the Pariah. This ceremony is called *kāppu*, காப்பு.

The name Vēlāttāḷ is commonly explained as mother of Subrahmaṇya, from Vēḷ and Āttāḷ. Nāgāttāḷ is regarded to signify the same from Nāgan (Subrahmaṇya) and Āttāḷ. Some Tamil scholars however do not favor this explanation. When revered in these forms Pārvatī or Kanyākumārī is regarded as a Pariah woman or Mātaṅgī.

The Pariahs enjoy even now, in many places, privileges, the origin of which cannot be explained except by admitting the existence of substantial reasons, which have long been forgotten. A Pariah ties to this day the tāli round the neck of Ēgāttāḷ, the tutelary goddess of Black Town in Madras. The Pariah, who acts as the bridegroom, arrives at the temple about ten days before the feast commences and is treated as described above. At *Perambūr*, near Madras, the same deity is called *Cēmāttāḷ*, mother of safety. In Mysore a Holiya is generally the priest of the village goddess, and the Kulvādi or Pariah headman of the village community iș regarded as the real proprietor of the village. At Mēlkōṭa a Holiya presents to Celvapiḷḷai, or utsava-idol, which is thus called as it is carried in procession at the festival, a branch of the Cami or Vahni tree to be used as an arrow for his bow at the hunting festival (*pārivēṭṭai*), and while the idol is moving in procession, a Pariah huntsman lets a hare run across the road in front of the car that the god may shoot at it; this done, the idol returns in grand procession to the temple. The Pariah receives as a reward (*pāritōṣikam*) a garland, the flowers of which are distributed among the heads of the large conflux of Pariahs. This hunting festival is in Malayālam called *paḷḷiveṭṭa*, or royal hunt. It is just possible that *pāri* and *paḷḷi* are identical words. The Holiyas pull the car at Mēlkōṭa and are not debarred from approaching it. They pull also the ropes of the cars at Kāñcipuram, Kumbhakōnam, Śrīvalliputtūr, and other places. In fact they do so wherever there are big temples. To obviate any unpleasantness arising on such occasions, it is laid down, as a rule, that the touch of Pariahs and outcastes who come to revere the deity does not pollute.

Dēvālayasamīpasthān dēvasēvārtham āgatān
Caṇḍālān patitān vāpi spṛṣṭvā na snānam ācarēt.[52]

The Holiyas are permitted in Mēlkōṭa to enter the Tirunārāyaṇa temple on three days of the year. The Brahmans ascribe this privilege to the circumstance that a poor but pious Pariah had observed that a cow approached every day a white ant's hole and let her milk drop into it. He searched and discovered that the image of Celvapiḷḷai was concealed in it. In consequence, the Pariah took compassion on the cow

[52] One need not bathe if one touches Caṇḍālas or outcastes, who stand near the temple and have come to worship God.

and supplied her daily with fodder. The great Vaiṣṇava reformer, Bhagavat Rāmānujācārya, had at the same time been dreaming of this Celvapiḷḷai image, and the Pariah showed it to him. As a reward for this act of piety, Rāmānujācārya allowed the Pariahs to enter the temple in future for three days of the year. Others say that this favor was granted because the Pariahs had protected him in their paṟaicēri, when he was pursued. Very likely, the privilege is of older origin. A similar custom prevails in *Kadiri*.[53]

It is most peculiar that the origin of the famous Jagannātha temple is also closely connected with the low-caste Pariahs. A *Śavara* mountaineer, called *Bāsu*, worshipped in secret the blue stone image of Jagannātha, to obtain which the powerful king of Mālva, Indradyumna, had despatched Brahmans to all quarters of the world. One of them penetrated at last into the wilderness where Bāsu lived. Bāsu detained the Brahman, made him marry his daughter, and led him after some time blindfolded to the place where the image of Jagannātha was lying concealed. The Brahman

---

[53] Compare "Archæological Notes," by M. J. Walhouse in the *Indian Antiquary*, vol. III, 1874, p. 191: "It is well known that the servile castes in Southern India once held far higher positions, and were indeed masters of the land on the arrival of the Brahmanical caste. Many curious vestiges of their ancient power still survive in the shape of certain privileges, which are jealously cherished, and, their origin being forgotten, are much misunderstood. These privileges are remarkable instances of survivals from an extinct order of society—shadows of long-departed supremacy, bearing witness to a period when the present haughty high-caste races were suppliants before the ancestors of degraded classes whose touch is now regarded as pollution. At Melkotta, the chief seat of the followers of Rāmanuja Achārya, and at the Brahmaṇ temple at Bailur, the Holeyars or Pareyars have the right of entering the temple on three days in the year, specially set apart for them. At the 'bull-games' at Dindigal, in the Madura district, which have some resemblance to Spanish bull-fights, and are very solemn celebrations, the Kallār, or robber caste, can alone officiate as priests and consult the presiding deity. On this occasion they hold quite a Saturnalia of lordship and arrogance over the Brāhmaṇs. In the great festival of Śiva at Trivalūr, in Tanjore the head-man of the Pareyars is mounted on the elephant with the god, and carries his *chauri*. In Madras, at the annual festival of the goddess of the Black Town, when a *tāli* is tied round the neck of the idol *in the*

worshipped the god, and, after the lapse of some time, was able to communicate his discovery to the king. As the king was very proud of his power, the god Jagannātha, in order to punish his pride, did allow him to build the temple, but did not manifest himself personally to Indradyumna. This favor was granted him after prolonged delay, and it was only with the help of the Śavara Bāsu that the image could finally be obtained and removed. Until very recently, pilgrims of all castes and outcastes frequented Puri and partook together of their meals, as the presence of Jagannātha is said to destroy all distinctions of caste, race, and faith; but now out-castes are no longer allowed to enter the sanctuary and to join in the eating of holy food, though the food prepared and sanctified at Puri can be eaten by Brahmans anywhere, even in the presence of the lowest people. The descendants of Bāsu are thus debarred from worshipping personally their own divinity.

Many Pariahs have attained high renown as poets and saints. Take for example, *Tiruvaḻḻuva Nāyanār*, the author

---

name of the entire community, a Pareyar is chosen to represent the bridegroom. In Madras, too, the mercantile caste, and in Vizagapatam the Brāhmaṇs, had to go through the form of asking the consent of the lowest castes to their marriages, though the custom has not died out." See Mr. J. D. B. Gribble's *Manual of Cuddapah*, p. 241.

See *Comparative Grammar of the Dravidian Languages* by Bishop Caldwell, second edition, p. 548: "Thus, at the annual festival of Ēgattaḷ, the only mother—a form of Kalī, and the tutelary goddess of the 'Black Town' of Madras—when a *tāli*, or bridal necklace (answering to our wedding ring), was tied round the neck of the idol in the name of the entire community, a Pareiya used to be chosen to represent the people as the goddess' bridegroom."

I am indebted to the Rev. H. Jensen of the Danish Lutheran Mission for my statement concerning the continuation of the service of a Pariah at the Ēgattaḷ temple in Black Town.

Major J S. F. Mackenzie has contributed on p. 36 of volume VIII of the *Indian Antiquary* an article on the "Customs of the Comti Caste." Most of the statements that note contains I have repeatedly heard in Madras, and I myself possess some documents confirming them. I quote this subject here merely as it ought not to be entirely omitted, and as it affords strong evidence of the great influence and authority once enjoyed by the now-despised Pariahs—an influence which apparently is exercised even at the present time.

of the Kuṟal and his so-called sister, the famous poetess, *Avvai*, the Vaiṣṇava Āḻvār *Tirupāṇ*, the author of the work beginning with *Amalan Ādipirān*, who was brought up by Pariahs, and the Śaiva saint *Nandan*, who was a Pariah. A Kurumba robber, *Tirumaṅgaimannan*, became afterwards a celebrated Vaiṣṇava Āḻvār.

These and many other instances can be adduced to prove the once flourishing condition of the now despised lowest classes.

Wrong Derivation of the term Holeya and Pulaya.

The Telugu Pariahs are called Mālavāṇḍlu, its corresponding term in Tamil *Mālar* is often used in the sense of Pulaiyar and equivalent to Paraiyar. The word Māla, in the sense of mountaineer or barbarian, occurs in Sanskrit. As the word *holeya* is derived from *hole*, ಹೊಲೆ, pollution, and the South-Indian *Pulayan* from *pula*, പുല, pollution, so also is Malaya occasionally derived from the Sanskrit *mala*, taint. All these derivations rest on no substantial philological grounds. They have been suggested by the accidental resemblance existing between the Sanskrit words *mala*, taint, and *pala*, flesh, and the Dravidian *pula* (*hole*), pollution, and their derivatives on the one side and the names of the *Mallas* or *Pallas* on the other side, and are used to revile and as an excuse for despising the low defenceless and ill-treated population.[54]

This tendency to revile strangers, enemies or slaves is, however, not confined to any particular country. *The Tatars*, when they first invaded Europe, were called Tartars, because they were supposed to have come from *Tartarus* or hell.

I further believe that all such Sanskrit words as *malla*, *māla*, *malaya*, *palli*, *&c.*, which are connected with the name

---

[54] Mr. Lewis Rice in his *Mysore and Coorg*, vol. I, p. 312, ventures another derivation : "the Holayar, whose name may be derived from *hola*, a field."

of the Mallas and Pallas, to have been introduced into that language from Dravidian.

Caste distinctions among Pariahs; Right and Left Hand Castes.

The Pariah caste is divided into 18 classes[55] like the Veḷḷāḷar, as has been already intimated. The first class of the Pariahs is called the Vaḷḷuvappaṟai. The highest caste of the Pulayar in Cochin also bears the name of Vaḷḷuva. One great cause that keeps the Pariahs and the Paḷḷar apart, or that prevents them from being on friendly terms with each other, is the fact that they take different sides in the great question of *right-hand* and *left-hand* castes.

The reference to this distinction necessitates some remarks. The cause of the division into *right-hand* and *left-hand* castes, and the time when this difference arose, are both unknown, though weighty reasons can be adduced against assigning to it a very early period. The legendary reports abound with suspicious details which militate against their trustworthiness. The contest seems to have been both national and religious.[56]

---

[55] Dr. Winslow enumerates in his *Tamil-English Dictionary* the following classes among the Pariahs: The Vaḷḷuvappaṟai, Tātappaṟai, Taṅkalānpaṟai, Tuṟcālippaṟai, Kuḷippaṟai, Tippaṟai, Muracappaṟai, Moṭṭappaṟai, Ampuppaṟai, Vaṭukappaṟai, Āliyappaṟai, Kōliyappaṟai, Vaḷippaṟai, Veṭṭiyarppaṟai, Caṅkuppaṟai. Compare Mr. J. H. Nelson's *Manual of Madura*, III, pp. 75–79. Mr. W. F. Sinclair says in the *Indian Antiquary*, vol. III, p. 130: "The *Parwāris* should not by rights be called outcastes, seeing that they have caste of their own, obey its rules, and squabble among themselves for precedence with a pertinacity worthy of ambassadors."

[56] In the edition of a portion of the Kuṟaḷ which was published together with an English translation and valuable notes by one of the earliest and best European Tamil Scholars, the late Mr. T, W, Ellis, of the Madras Civil Service, is found on page 44 the following passage: "Intercourse with foreign nations, the extension of commerce, and other circumstances have in latter times materially altered the manners of the olden time and infringed the privileges of the landed proprietors, but they have not been able to prevent a lively tradition of them remaining, and this has given origin to the dissensions between the factions denominated *Valang-caiyār* and *Idung-caiyār*,

The five classes of artisans—the carpenters; goldsmiths, blacksmiths, braziers, and masons, well known in Southern India as *Pañcāḷar* or *Kammāḷar*—regard themselves as the real Brahmans and, as the descendants of the divine artificer *Viśvakarma*, call themselves Viśva Brahmans. They assume the title of *Ācārya*, wear the holy thread, and claim the right to perform religious ceremonies among themselves, especially at marriages. They further declare that there were originally five Vēdas, but that *Vēda Vyāsa*, in order to curtail their privileges, suppressed the fifth and arranged the other four in such a manner as suited Vyāsa and the false Brahmans whom he headed; that he tried to win the reigning king over to his side, and, when he did not succeed, that he instigated the king's murder and placed an illegitimate son on the throne, who conferred on Vyāsa the dignity of priest of the royal family. According to one version Vyāsa induced the king to issue a proclamation, enacting that all those who sided with the king should be styled right-hand caste men, and all those who opposed him left-hand caste men. Another tradition asserts that Vyāsa's right hand was cut off by a bigoted Śaiva, who heard Vyāsa swear with his uplifted right hand that Viṣṇu was superior to Śiva and that he had never in his Purāṇas opposed Viṣṇu.[57] Others transfer these

---

or, as commonly though improperly called, *the right and left hand castes*; the former including the whole of the agricultural tribes, who endeavour, under a different order of things, to maintain their ancient pre-eminence; the latter, including chiefly the trading and manufacturing tribes, who endeavour, and in modern days generally with success, to evade it."—According to the late Dr. Burnell (see *Indian Antiquary*, vol. II, (1873), p. 274): "The distinction arises primarily from the landowners and their serfs being the heads of one class, and the Brahmans, artizans, and other interlopers forming the other. But the constituent castes of either party vary." The Pañcālas or Kammāḷar are known in Tamil by the title of *Ācāri* ஆசாரி.

So far as I am informed, and as I have stated above, the Brahmans are not included in either faction, though some lists mention them as partisans.

[57] Compare the *Decision of the Cittūr Jillā Court* (చిత్తూరు జిల్లా అదాల తుకోర్టు తీర్పు) printed at Cittūr, 1881, on these dissensions. An account

events to Kāñcipuram, and declare that, when the two opposed parties brought their complaints before the Pallava king reigning over the Cōla country, the Kammāḷar, Bēri Ceṭṭies and their friends were sitting on the left hand of the king and the Veḷḷāḷar and their adherents on the right hand. The left-hand side is regarded by the Kammāḷar as the place of honor.

---

is given on page 29 of the circumstances in which Vyāsa lost his hand. His opponent is in this Cittūr Decision described as వీరముష్టియైన అతడు. *Vīramuṣṭi* means a Vīra Śaiva or Jaṅgama, who precedes a procession, holding a shield and brandishing a sword. He is also called Vṛṣabhēśvara. The Skandapurāṇa contains also the story about the cutting off of Vyāsa's arm. Captain J. S. T. Mackenzie connects the *Vyasanu-tōlu Kallu* (Vyasana's armstone) found in Mysore with this event. Compare *Indian Antiquary*, vol. II, (1873), p. 49.

As the Pañcalar claim the privilege of being their own priests and the Brahmans oppose this claim, many disputes and even serious disturbances of the public peace have ensued. Such was the case, *e.g.*, at Cittūr in 1817. Through the kindness of the present Judge at Cittūr, Mr. Crole, I have obtained a copy of the judgment from which I give the following extracts:

After mentioning the names of the plaintiffs and the six defendants it begins: "1. This suit was brought against the defendants by the plaintiffs to recover Rs. 530¼ damages on account of the defendants having prevented the plaintiffs from celebrating a marriage in their family.

"The record consists of the plaint, three answers, one reply and two rejoinders . . . 2. The plaintiffs in this suit call themselves Kammālars, the descendants of five Brahmas. The Kammalars follow five crafts, namely, that of carpenter, blacksmith, goldsmith, mason and brass-smith. 3. The plaintiffs state that they and their tribe have been accustomed, and that they consider themselves entitled, and have resolved, to conduct their own marriages, and other domestic and religious ceremonies without the interference of the Brahmins, to which tribe the defendants belong. The plaintiffs maintain that one of their own tribe is their *Guru*, and performs their religious rites, and that they will not attend to, nor employ a Brahmin therein, and they state their confidence that no Court of Justice can give the defendants or Brahmins liberty to enter their houses by force to officiate at their ceremonies, moreover, they state that they are neither of the Vaisya nor Sudra tribes, but are descendants of Brahma and that therefore they do not require Brahmins to officiate for them. That moreover they, the plaintiffs are Deva, or divine Brahmins, and that the defendants are *Go* or cow Brahmins who were originally Sudras, and by certain penance and ceremonies obtained Brahminism, and that they, the plaintiffs, can prove their right from the Veda, Smriti and Vasishthapurānum and the Silpa Sāstram. 4. The principal defendants, namely, the 1st, 2nd, 3rd, 4th and 5th maintain that they are Brahmins of the Siva Bhakti and have a right to perform the ceremonies

The charge of having suppressed the fifth Vēda is very extraordinary indeed, especially if one considers that the original number of the Vēdas is indicated by the name *Trayī*, or Trinity, representing the Ṛg, Yajur and Sāma Vēdas, and that the fourth or Atharvavēda is generally ascribed to a later period. The existence and destruction of a fifth Vêda, assuming such a work to have ever existed, must therefore be assigned to a comparatively late or modern time.

---

and religious rites of the plaintiffs who they state to be Sankaras, or outcastes of the Sudra tribe. The defendants in consequence deny that the plaintiffs could ever become Brahmins, though they were born again ever so many times. Moreover that if the plaintiffs think proper to perform the marriage and other ceremonies using forms of prayers taken from the Veda they will not only be liable to suffer a great punishment in their next birth, but to be punished criminally by the executors of the law appointed by Government, who they state would never suffer the plaintiffs to perform any ceremonies contrary to the law of their sect, to ascertain which the defendants request that the opinion of the law officer of the Court may be taken on the subject. 5. The above is the sum of the difference between the parties. . . 9. The evidence in this case is very long and contradictory, but the Court has no doubt from a consideration thereof but that the defendants did actually, seriously and violently molest the plaintiffs in the celebration of a marriage which the plaintiffs were celebrating though they (the defendants) did not actually prevent it, as the marriage took place notwithstanding their interference, though not without the plaintiffs meeting with much obstruction from the defendants. 10. It is a notorious fact which the plaintiff's witnesses have deposed to, that the plaintiffs and persons of the Kammalar caste (like Kannadiyar, Satânis and Jainas) do frequently celebrate their religious festivals without calling in the Brahmins of any other sect to aid them in the performance of any part thereof. The plaintiffs have declared that they admit those marriages only to be perfectly regular, which are celebrated by Gurus of their own appointment. They do not admit the superiority of any othor tribe to themselves. These opinions they state to be according to the Hindu Sâstra, but it is a point and a right, which it is well known the Siva and Vishnu Brahmins do not admit, and therefore it has not been considered necessary to consult on this subject the pandits of the Courts, no more than if it were a question of law regarding a religious difference between any other sect and the Brahmins, on which they never would agree. If the plaintiffs, who deny the superiority of the defendants as Brahmins do in their tribe choose to follow or relinquish any ancient custom or to establish any new ceremony which is not contrary to honesty, decorum, and tho peace of the country, neither the defendants nor any other persons have any right to interfere, nor would the officers of Government

The division of the population into right-hand and left-hand castes occurred most likely simultaneously with the religious agitation which introduced into Southern India the now prevailing Brahmanical supremacy. The imminent decay of the Jaina power opened a fair prospect to the Brahmans of which they were not slow to take advantage. They gathered round them their followers, while their opponents, who represented in certain respects the national party, did the same. This movement seems to have been originally

---

ever interfere, if it should not appear to be necessary for the peace of the country. It appears that marriages celebrated by Gurus of the plaintiffs own sect have been for a long period at least admitted by a very great body (if not perhaps by the whole) of them, and at all events are now by them acknowledged to be good and proper and valid, and according to *their* interpretation of the Sastra perfectly conformable thereto. No other sects therefore have any right to interfere, especially a sect (namely that of the defendants or Smarta Brahmins) which the plaintiffs do not acknowledge to be superior to them; for the plaintiffs' rejection of them (the defendants, the Smarta Brahmins) as their spiritual guides or Gurus is what the defendants themselves acknowledge that any Hindu is at liberty to do. Thousands among themselves (the Smarta Brahmins) have of late years left them and from being Siva bhaktars have become Vishnu bhaktars, and have consequently chosen the Gurus of another sect to be their Gurus. Had the plaintiffs introduced ever so many innovations into their ceremonies (which they do not appear to have done), as they do not admit that the defendants have any more concern with them (the plaintiffs) than they (the plaintiffs) have with the defendants (Brahmins), the latter had no business to go near them on the occasion of the celebration of their marriage. They (the defendants) have no right to force themselves as Purohitas upon any tribe who do not acknowledge them, as their superiors, and Purohitas. In the opinion of the Courts the plaintiffs were, and are, fully entitled to perform (the marriage in question or any other) their religious ceremonies in such a manner as the tribe to which they belong may from time to time establish to be the rule and form of their caste, and it is so decreed accordingly . . . Given under my hand and the seal of the Court this twenty-eighth day of June in the year of our Lord one thousand eight hundred and twenty.

(Signed) JOSEPH DACRE,

Judge."

In 1843 a similar case was tried in Salem before a Brahman, N. Krishnamâchâryulu . . . A Pañcâlan, Râmalingâchâri, for claiming certain rights, had been insulted and severely beaten by some persons, and his sacred thread had also been torn to pieces. The defendants pleaded that Râmalingâchâri, as belonging to the Goldsmith caste (or *Kamsalajâti* in Telugu) had no right to study the Vêda and to undertake any Prâyaścitta, or any other religious cere-

confined to Southern India, its centre being at Kāñcipuram, the seat of so many religious and political dissensions, where there are to this day special halls for both parties, called Valaṅkai-maṇṭapams and Itaṅkai-maṇṭapams.[58] As the Paḷḷar and the Pariahs belong to different hands and the Vaḷḷuvar are the priests of both, the division into right-hand and left-hand castes must very probably have taken place after the Vaḷḷuvar had obtained this position. At the time of *Bhagavat Rāmānujācārya* this division into right-hand and left-hand castes was already an acknowledged institution, as different hours were assigned to right and left hand people for entering the Celvapiḷḷai temple at *Mēlkōṭa*, which place is also called *Patitapāvanakṣētra*, *i.e.*, the field where even outcastes can be purified. The influence of the Jainas was perhaps strongest in towns where the artisan classes form an important and powerful portion of the population, while the Brahmans appealed to the land-owning and agricultural classes, whom they won over by entreaties or by threats. The Brahmans have not joined and strictly speaking do not belong to either side, but their interests lie mainly with the right side. As in various localities the same castes have embraced different sides, it is difficult to assign to all a permanent position. Yet, on the whole, the principal parties on both sides are always the same.[59]

---

mony, whose performance is a privilege of the Brahmans, and that the Kamsalajati ranked according to the Dharmasāstra among the Grāmacaṇḍalas. The Court concurred in this view and the case was dismissed, Rāmaliṅgachari paying costs. See *Sēlam Jillā Tīrmānavu*, Madras, 1886.

[58] On p. 326 of the *Jātisangrahasāra* (in Tamil ஜாதிசங்கிரகசாரம்) is mentioned a copperplate order or *Tāmraśāsanam* which confirms the position of the Vanniyar, they held at Kāñci during the reign of *Sukhakalyāṇa* in the 762nd year of Śalivahana Śaka; but, though it is stated there, that this Śāsanam is still preserved, no one seems ever to have seen it.

[59] The quarrels and actual fights which occurred between these hostile parties have given rise to much litigation before Magistrates and Judges, especially in the Chingleput and North-Arcot districts. The judgment of George Coleman, Judge and Magistrate of Chingleput, dated the 25th July

This dissension must have seriously affected, for some time at least, the agricultural, mechanical, and commercial interests of the country, for, as both parties were stubborn, a great deal of inconvenience must have been felt, till each party was able to supply its own wants. The right-hand side had in these circumstances to seek a fresh supply of artisans until the necessary knowledge was acquired by men in its own ranks. Some who joined it were perhaps deserters from

---

1809, specifies the different people of both hands, gives their emblems, flags and instruments, and fixes certain privileges.

I have applied to the Court and gone to Chingleput with the express purpose to obtain a copy of this important judgment from the District Court, but it could not be found among the records, though many decisions of less consequence and of earlier years are still extant.

However, through the exertions of Mr. A. Krishnasvamy Iyer, B.A., an official of the Accountant-General's Office, and a much esteemed former pupil of mine, I have been able to secure a Tamil manuscript copy of the judgment. On the *right hand* are enumerated the *Vēḷāḷar* and *Kavaraikaḷ* with the following insignia: white umbrella, white flag, curved fan, chowry, arukuṭṭivaṭṭi, plough, plough-flag, monkey-flag, cuckoo-flag, parrot-flag, bell, conch, wheel stick, big-drum, green, blue lotus garland, *Ātti* flag, *Tavaṇṭai*, trumpet; 2, *Vatuka Vēḷāḷar* (Northern or Telugu Veḷḷaḷar) with swan flag; 3, *Reḍḍikaḷ* with plough flag; 4, *Kammavārukaḷ* (agricultural labourers) with bull-flag; 5, *Kontaḷavarkaḷ* with chakora flag; 6, *Nattamān* with Āḷi flag; 7 *Malaiyamān* with *Aritāḷa* or *Śrītala* flag; 8 *Kōmaṭṭikaḷ* (merchants) with cotton-flag, *Makaratōraṇam*-drum, Vimumayir, Iṭṭimuracu; 9, *Iṭaiyar* (shepherds) with wheel; 10, *Vaṭuka Iṭaiyar* (Telugu shepherds) with conch; 11, *Kaṇṇiṭaiyar* (Kanarese shepherds), with tent, . . . five-coloured flag; 12, *Patmacāliyar* (weavers) with tiger vehicle, male tiger flag; 13, *Paṭṭucāliyar* (silk weavers) with two-headed bird flag; 14, *Vaṭukacēṇiyar* (northern weavers) with jasmine flag, Nākapācam, five-coloured flag; 15, *Jāṇṭravar* (Telugu weavers) with crocodile; 16, *Kaṇṇiṭaiya-Cēniyar* (Kanarese weavers) with wild jasmine garland, big eagle flag, Vicurutaṇṭai; 17, *Paṭṭunūlkāṟar* (silk thread weavers) with silk flag; 18, *Cēṭar* (weavers) with tortoise flag, and *Koḷiñci* flag; 19, *Cēkkuvāṇiyar* (oilpress mongers) with ceḍaiceṭi (ceṇṭu-toṇṭu), eḷḷurāci, sesamum-leaf garland, garuḍa-flag, drum; 20, *Iḷaivāṇiyar* (leaf oil-mongers) with kovai-garland, drum, cuckoo flag; 21, *Oṇṭi erutu vāṇniyar* (one bullock oil-mongers) with five-coloured parrot flag; 22, *Jaṇappar* (hemp dressers) with chowry flag; 23, *Mucciyar* (painters, &c.,) with makara flag; 24, *Kāñciyar* (braziers) with Poti flag; 25, *Vētakārar* (basketmakers) with Cikkiri flag, wooden-legged horse, sword flag; 26, *Nari cōkiyar* (Fox-beggars) with dog flag; 27, *Tamiḻ Kucavar* (potters), *Vaṭuka Kucavar* (Telugu potters), *Kuca Kaṇakkar*; 28, *Mēḷakkāṟar* (flooters) with drum flag; 29, *Naṭṭuvar* (dancing masters) with cymbal flag; 30, *Dācikaḷ*

the hostile camp, while others were outsiders, Muhammadan artisans, for instance, who were allowed to earn their living in the Hindu community by following their profession.

The fifth caste formed of outcastes is in consequence of this dissension divided into two great hostile camps, on the right side are ranged the Pariahs, and on the left side the Cakkilis or leather-workers. It appears that there prevails in some parts of the South the peculiar phrase: " the Pariahs

---

(dancing girls) with Manmatha flag; 31, *Cāṇār* and *Īḻar* (toddy-drawers) with kuriñci flag, knife and ladder; 32, *Kuṟavar* (mountaineers, foresters, snake-catchers, basketmakers, salt-sellers), with donkey flag; 33, *Cukkār ceṭṭi lampāṭikaḷ* (salt-sellers) with picturesque flag; 34, *Vēṭṭakkārar* (hunters) with sling flag; 35, *Paṭṭanavar* (?) with tortoise flag; 36, *Karaiyar* (sea-coastmen) with fish flag; 37, *Oṭṭar* (road-makers and tank-diggers from Orissa) with spade flag; 38, *Uppaṟavar* (common tank-diggers) with pig flag; 39, *Pōyi* (bearers) with palanquin flag; 40, Paṇiceyvōrkaḷ (?) (menial servants?) with Tārai (trumpet) flag; 41, *Tamiḻ Vaṇṇār* and *Vaṭuka Vaṇṇār* (Tamil and Telugu washermen) with curved knife, lotus garland and white elephant; 42, *Tamiḻ Nāvitar* (Tamil barbers) with tumpai garland, animal with human face; 43, *Vaṭuka Nāvitar* (Telugu barbers) with nākasaram (musical instrument); 44, *Tompuravar* (rope-dancers) with Keṭai flag; 45, *Māriyamman Pucārikaḷ* (Māriyamman priests) with small drum flag; 46, *Pucārikaḷ* with hollow brass ring flag; 47, *Iruḷar* (wild foresters) with iron bar flag; 48, *Arippukkār Kavarai* (kavarai weavers) with lotus flag; 49, *Vaṭuka Paṇḍāram* (northern mendicants) with battle-axe flag; 50, *Vañcūrār* (?) with pearl flag; 51, *Kuṭukuṭuppaikāraḷ* (soothsaying beggars) with sākti flag; 52, *Enāti* (forestmen) with hare flag; 53, *Kalācukāṟar* (lascars) with cart flag; 54, *Veḷikkarumār* excommunicated blacksmiths) with bellows and hammer flag; 55, *Veḷikal taccar* (excommunicated carpenters) with chisel flag; 56, *Kappal taccar* (ship carpenters) with adze flag; 57, *Kappal vaṭukar* (Telugu sailors) with ship flag; 58, *Paṇṭar* (bards) with sword flag.

The people and ensigns of the fifth class are – 1, *Pavuniyar* or *Paḷanikal* (processionists) with ḍamara (drum) flag; 2, *Vaḷḷuvar*, *Māvaṭṭiyār* and *Veṭṭiyār* (mahaut), *Paṟaiyar* and *Paṇṭapaṟaiyar* with white umbrella, white chowry, white flag, conch, vajra stick, trumpet (tamukku), drum (tappaṭṭai), paṅka (trumpet), tuttāri (short trumpet), big tuttāri, paṟaiya music, five pots and white makara (alligator) festoons.

The *left hand* musters 1, *Pēri Ceṭṭikaḷ* (*Bēri* merchants) with kite flag; 2, *Nakara Vāṇiyar* (town oil-mongers) with *toṇṭu* garland and garland of nine gems; 3, *Kaikkōḷar* (weavers) with tiruvaraipattiram, aḍakkam, lance, male vulture, lion flag, bear flag, deer flag, peacock flag, cuckoo flag, drum; 4, *Kammāḷar* (artisans). [This class is composed of the *Taṭṭār* (goldsmiths), *Kannār* (braziers), *Cirpar* (masons), *Kollar* (blacksmiths) and *Taccar* (car-are not left-hand people, they belong to the Tamils;" an expression whose exact meaning it is difficult to make out especially as a *Tamilan* or Tamulian denotes, in Madras, a Hindu in general, and not a Pariah.[60] I believe that the meaning of this phrase is that, as the Tamilar or Vellālar, the masters of the Pariahs and principal Śūdras, are right hand men, so are their dependents, the Pariahs. The Pariahs enjoy

---

penters); the word Kammāla is most likely the Sanskrit Kammāra, which occurs already in the Vēda in the meaning of artificer.] With hammer, chisel, adze, compass or ulakaṇi, stick, parrot flag, eagle flag, or white kite flag; 5, *Pallikal* with big axe, crane feather, veṅkai garland, red lotus garland, crow flag, cloud-coloured flag, fire flag, cock flag, vulture flag, fox flag, date flag, stone flag, green flag, hair-queue flag, drum and bow, kuṇṭali, black flag.

As belonging to the fifth class of the Iṭaṅkai are mentioned—1, *Pallar* with nelli garland and crab flag; 2, *Cakkilikal* (leather-workers) with saffron screen, black garland, warrior sword, cocoa leaf, drum, curved stick.

Mr. Coleman's decision refers also to the manner in which temple, funeral and other processions should be performed by the different castes, but to quote his remarks here would lead us too far away.

The Government Oriental Manuscripts' Library contains two lists of the right and left hand castes. 98 different divisions are ascribed to each sect. If the lists had not been very inaccurate, I should have printed them here, but they place *inter alias* the *Kammālar* on the right-hand and the Brahmans on the left-hand.

Dr. Macleane (in the Administration Manual, vol. I, p. 69), though without producing confirmatory evidence, makes the important statement that the *male Pullies* belong to the right and the *female Pullies* to the left hand. He says: "The following lists show the more important of the castes "which take part in the disputes of the rival hands. On the left hand, "Chetties, artisans, oilmongers, weavers, Patnavar, male leather-workers, and "female Pullies. On the right hand; Vellaular, Cavarays, Comaties, account-"ants, silk-weavers, male Pullies, Pariahs and female leather-workers. "It is to be observed that the females of two of the inferior castes take differ-"ent sides from their husbands in these disputes." I have made inquiries among the Pallis on this point and they deny the correctness of the statement, yet it is very difficult to decide such a question, unless both sides produce their authorities. It must certainly appear peculiar that husband and wife should belong to the different rival hands, as if it were desirable to specially provide causes for domestic disagreements. Mr. Nelson has, as will be seen on the next page, made a similar statement concerning the Cakkilis in Madura.

[60] The Rev. E. Löventhal of Vellore communicated to me the existence of the saying: பறையர் இடங்கை அல்ல அவர்கள் தமிழர்; "The Pariyar are not left hand, they are Tamilians."

also the honorific title of *Valaṅkamattār* or *Valaṅkulattār* and claim in consequence precedence over the left-hand *Paḷḷar*.

The Tamil Cakkili, the Telugu and Kanarese Mādiga, and the Marātha *Māng* all do belong to the same caste. Their occupation is mostly connected with leather and rope making. The enmity between the common Pariahs and these people is very acrimonious as it concerns precedence; and a *Māng*, who as ropemaker is generally also the hangman, is said to regard as his proudest and most meritorious action the hanging of a Mahār or Marātha Pariah. Nevertheless, the Pariahs and the Cakkilis, when not actually engaged in hostilities, acknowledge each other in a friendly manner as brothers-in-law. In his Madura Manual (II, p. 7) Mr. Nelson mentions the curious fact that in Madura the Cakkili women belong to the right-hand and their husbands to the left-hand.

The words *Māng and Mādiga* are corruptions of *Mātaṅga*.

The division of the *Śakti* worshippers or *Śāktas* in Dakṣiṇācāris and Vāmācāris has nothing in common with the right or left hand castes. This difference concerns merely the pūjā, inasmuch as the *dakṣiṇācāra*, the right observance, allows only milk, fruit, cakes made of blackgram, and other sweetmeats and sweet drinks, while the *vāmācāra*, the left or adverse observance, permits, besides the mentioned eatables and drinks, meat and liquors also.

The Vaḷḷuvar.

The oppression which the Pariahs and Paḷḷar have suffered has not drawn them closer together, but yet these two classes have their priesthood in common. These priests are called Vaḷḷuvar, and their name has become renowned by *Tiru Vaḷḷuva Nāyanār*, the author of the famous Tamil work the Kuṛaḷ (குறள்). It is evident from this appellation itself, that Tiruvaḷḷuva Nāyanār is not the real name of this celebrated man, but only his title.[61] This poet, who was born and died at Mailapur, a suburb of Madras, showed in his writings a knowledge of, and a tendency towards Jainism; and though some deny the fact of his having been a Jain, other Vaḻḻuvar admit it: at all events the title Nāyanār may be taken in favor of such an assumption, as it is used by the Jains as an honorific appellation. The word means *lord* and *devotee,* and is probably a contracted form of the Tamil honorific term *Nāyakanār*, from which the syllable *ka* has been dropped. *Nāyaka*, a leader, especially a leader of troops, *i.e.*, a general, is derived from the Sanskrit *nī*, to lead. This word becomes in Tamil *Nāyakan* (Naik), in Telugu *Nāyaḍu* (Naiḍu), and in Malayālam *Nāyar* (Nair), and is used as a title by many Hindus in Southern India; it is adopted in the

---

[61] The accounts given about *Tiruvaḻḻuva Nāyanār* are very obscure. One fact alone is clear that he belonged to one of the lowest classes of the population, but that the highest classes could not ignore his talents, and to save their superiority connected his birth with the Brahman caste. Another important item of information is that other celebrated Tamil poets as *Kapilar* and *Avvai* are also brought into intimate contact with the same lower classes. The legend given below makes Kapilar, Avvai and Tiruvaḻḻuva Nāyanār, brothers and sister, though it is manifest that they did not all live and compose their works at the same time; still the connection of all with one another and with the Pariahs and Pulayar is very peculiar indeed.

Brahma performed, according to the legend, a sacrifice for the explanation of the Sanskrit and Tamil languages and *Agastya* arose from it out of a pot. The sage married the daughter of the Ocean, and had from her a son *Peruñcārakan*. His son married at Tiruvālūr a Pulaiyan woman or *Pulaicci*, and their offspring was *Bhagavan* (பகவன்). About this time there lived *Tavamuni*, a scion of the Brahmavaṁśa, who had married a Brahman woman *Aruḻmaṅkai*. They had a daughter, but left her behind to perform a sacrifice at the Virali mountain. A Pariah of Uraiyūr found the girl, and brought her up, until there fell a downpour of earth which killed all the inhabitants in the neighbourhood except the girl, who took refuge in the house of one *Nītiyappan* at Melūrakaram. On his way to Benares the young Bhagavan stopped at the choultry near Melūrakaram, when the girl passed. He asked her whether she was a Pulaicci or Valaicci, and beat her with a wooden ladle on her head, so that it bled, and the wound left eventually a scar. On his return from Benares the pilgrim stopped at the same inn and again saw the young girl, who had since become very beautiful, at the house of Nītiyappan, but he did not recognise her and asked her foster-father to give him his

same meaning by the Bhillālas, Mahārs and Gonds. The word *Valluvan* வள்ளுவன், (*Pl.* Valluvar) I take to mean "the honorable Palla;" Vallu or rather Pallu being the collective name of the Palla caste and *an* (*ar*) the honorific pronominal affix. The present position of the Valluvar is highly interesting. He is famous for his superior attainments in Astrology, and is much consulted when horoscopes are to be cast. Though socially an outcaste, he is respectfully treated by Brahmans and especially by Brahman ladies, who often have recourse to his advice. He wears the holy brahmanical thread or *yajñōpavīta*, in Tamil *pūṇunūl* or *pūṇūl*.[62] At the weddings of Pariahs and Pallar he utters Sanskrit passages

---

daughter in marriage. He consented and the marriage was celebrated when Bhagavan returned from Rāmēśvaram. On his anointing, according to the ceremonial, the head of his bride, he saw the scar on her head and recognised her as the girl he had beaten. Ashamed he ran away, but the girl—who was henceforth called Āti (ஆதி)—ran behind him. At Paṇaccēri she overtook him at last, when Bhagavan exacted from her the promise that she would leave behind her all the children which they might have on their journeys. She consented and much against her inclination kept her word, advised by her babies to do so. Thus were born *Avvai* (அவ்வை) or Auvai (ஔவை) as an incarnation of Sarasvatī, *Uppai* (உப்பை) in Toṇḍamaṇḍalam, *Atikamān* (அதிகமான்) in Karuvūr, *Uṟuvai* (உறுவை) in Kāvēripaṭṭanam, *Kapilar* (கபிலர்) in Tiruvārūr, *Valli* near the Vēli mountain and *Tiruvalluvar* in an oil nut tree tope at Mailapūr.

All these children play important parts in the legends and poetry of Southern India. *Avvai* was nursed by hunters. *Uppai* was brought up by washermen and married a Pariah grave-digger. They were very poor, and she was attacked by small-pox and went about covered only with margosa-tree leaves. Thus she became known and worshipped as Mariyamman. *Adīkamān* was educated by Ceraman, *Uṟuvai* by brewers, *Kapilar* by the Brahman *Pāpaiya*, and *Valli* by Kuṟavar. The names of *Tiruvalluvar* and of most of his so-called brothers and sisters are no proper names.

[62] *See* Ñānaveṭṭi (ஞானவெட்டி) ascribed to Tiruvalluva Nāyanār edited by Aruṇācala Mudaly, p. 9; stanza 40, which begins (பூணுநூல் தரித்துக்கொள்வோம் சிவ சிவ (Pūṇunūl tarittukkoḷvōm, Śiva, Śiva) "Let us wear the sacred thread, Śiva, Śiva, let us follow the promptings of the five senses; let us carry all the insignia, especially the white umbrellas and white chowries, as well as the golden fans used by the gods and sages, beautiful marks and clothes. Let us praise by worshipping the beginning and ending of Ōm, in which lustre of wisdom and divine essence are manifest."

in the marriage ceremonial, the meaning of which he probably does not know. Considering how jealous the Brahman priests are of keeping secret their sacred verses, it is very strange indeed that the Vaḻḻuvar knows and uses some of them. This knowledge must have been acquired long ago, perhaps at a time when friendly relations still existed between the Brahman settlers and the original population.

He is most probably the representative of the ruling class of ancient times, and his name can still be easily discerned, as it is preserved in historical records and geographical accounts. I need only mention the *Vaḻḻuvakōn*, of Vaḻḻuvanāḍu, the king of the Vaḻḻuvar, who presided at the great assembly of Kēraḷam, when a new Perumāl was chosen every twelfth year to rule over the whole of Malayāḷam. I pointed out some years ago the connection which exists between the Vaḻḻuvar and Pallavas and shall recur to this question later on.

All this splendour of the Vaḻḻuvan has departed and he is now known only as the priest of the Pariahs and Paḻḻar. He occupies the highest position among the Pariahs, while his name connects him with the Paḻḻar, and among the kindred of the latter, *i.e.*, among the Pulayar of Cochin, the Vaḻḻuvar still rank highest. We may perhaps be justified in regarding him as representing a link between the first and second Dravidian stage.

This suggestion will naturally be repudiated by the Vaḻḻuvar, for they regard themselves as much superior to the people committed to their spiritual charge.

To accept the assertions of every individual Hindu would be to admit a separate creation for each tribe, sect, trade, profession, and calling. The pride of caste, even among the lowest in the country, the tendency towards exclusiveness, and the firm belief in individual superiority combined with a strong spirit of conservatism, divide the Indian population into innumerable sections. And as if the existing distinctions did not suffice, new conditions and new complications are continually giving rise to new variations and combinations in Hindu society. Thus among the Vellālar, such new castes have lately arisen, and, if I am not mistaken, some promoters of the widow-remarriage movement advocate the establishment of a new caste, composed of those who have married widows and of the offspring of such marriages.

CHAPTER V.

On the Pallar, Pallavas, Pulayar, Ballas (Bhallas), Bhīls, Pulindas, &c.

What was originally an accidental discrepancy in the pronunciation of the name of the Mallas or Pallas, though immaterial in itself, has produced occasionally in the course of time a real difference. It may perhaps be assumed, either that those who had descended from the mountains to the plains preferred to be called Pallas, because the Dravidian word *pallam* signifies *depth* or *low country*, or that they imparted this meaning to the term *pallam*, unless the vocal similarity between *Pallan*, a Palla, and *pallam*, low country, is regarded as an accidental freak of language.

In these circumstances one may be justified in distinguishing in certain localities, between the Mallas and Pallas as between Highlanders and Lowlanders, while we may find elsewhere Mallas living in the plains and Pallas on the mountains. After a prolonged residence of the descendants of the Highlanders in the plains and of the Lowlanders in the mountains, both might re-adjust their names to the actual places they are occupying, and call themselves, respectively, Mallar and Pallar.

The Pallas appear in Sanskrit literature as *Pallavas*, *Pahlavas*, *Pahnavas*, *Palhava* and *Plavas*.

The formation of the word *Pallava*[63] can be explained in different ways. It may have been derived from the word *Palla* which, being combined with the pronominal affix *an*, formed the honorific term *Paḻḻavan*, and eventually dropped the final *n*; or, if of Sanskrit origin, the affix *va* may either have been added to Palla, or the Taddhita affix *a* to the term Paḻḻu, which denotes the Paḻḻar caste as an aggregate. In the latter case *Pallava* would have been formed from *Pallu* and ought to have been *Pāllava*, but according to Pāṇini V, 2, 127 (*arśa ādibhyo'c*) Vṛddhi or long *a* is not necessary.

The omission of one *l* and the insertion in its place of an *h* requires a few remarks in order to connect *Palhava*, *Pahlava* and *Puhnava* with *Palla*, which was no doubt the original Dravidian form with which the Aryans became first acquainted.

Before a language reaches the literary stage, dialectical differences excepted, only one form of speech does generally prevail, which is the language in common use, the popular or *Prākrit* idiom. In course of time, with the growth of literature, the language, or rather the literary speech, becomes more and more settled and stationary, and certain formations, owing to their having been preferred by poets and other authors, are widely adopted and supersede those previously used. The refined or *Sanskrit* language must have originated in some such manner. Its very existence presupposes the *Prākrit*, as the original Prākrit must be older than the later *Sanskrit*. The so-called Prākrit forms, which are found, *e.g.*, in the Vedic literature, should not for this reason be regarded as belonging to a later period, simply because they belong to Prākrit, as they may even represent

---

63 The *Jātisaṅgrahasāra* on p. 171 says that *Pallavan* is derived from *Puravalan*, one who has got the strength of body, that *pura* was dropped in course of time, *V* changed into *P*, and *van* added.

the older Prākrit phase.[61] While Prākrit is indefinite, Sanskrit is definite and becomes in consequence ossified and unchangeable. Eventually it loses its hold on the people, but remains the linguistic standard of the educated and the dialect of the learned. It supplies in its turn the material for a modern Prākrit, which may likewise contain some relics of the original Prākrit, but from which, as prior to Sanskrit, it must be distinguished.

Applying these remarks to the special subject before us, it is not at all impossible that, as the Gaudian *Kaṇḍa* has been changed in Sanskrit into *Khaṇḍa,* similarly the original Dravidian and ancient Prākrit word *Palla* has been already at an early date altered and become *Palha* and *Pahla,* which three different terms were then in use at one and the same time. Sanskrit prefers on the whole a form whose pronunciation is more difficult than what satisfies the Dravidian languages. Some of these changes may have been made for reasons of which we are now ignorant. In support of my supposition that *Palha* or *Pahla* is a modification of *Palla,* I contend that a similar connection does apparently exist between the names *Kalhaṇa* or *Kahlaṇa* and *Kalla ;* between *Balhaṇa, Balhi, Balhika, Balhīka, Bālhi,* &c., or *Bahlaṇa, Bahli, Bahlikā, Bahlīka, Bāhli,* &c., and *Balla ;* between *Bilhaṇa* (*Vilhaṇa*) or *Bihlaṇa* (*Vihlaṇa*) and *Billa,* (*Villa*) *;* between *Malhaṇa* or *Mahlaṇa* and *Malla ;* between *Śilhana* or *Śihlana* and *Śilla ;* and between *Sulhaṇa, Suhlaṇa* or *Sullaṇa* and an original *Sulla.* The names ending in *ṇ* like Balhaṇa, Kalhaṇa, Malhaṇa and Sulhana have some resemblance with those Dravidian names ending in *aṇṇa,* as Rāghaṇṇa, Nāgaṇṇa, &c. Of the change of double *l* into *lh*, the change of *Mallāri* into *Malhāri* in Marāṭhi affords an example.

---

[61] For instance compare *kṛikalāsa* with *kṛikaddāśu, purōḍāśa* with *purōlāśa, kṣullaka* with kṣudraka and *bhallākṣa* with *bhadrākṣa,* in Professor A. Weber's *Indische Studien,* II, p. 87, note.

The introduction of an *h* into words in which it originally found no place has already been commented upon when discussing on p. 61 the origin of the names *Mhār* and *Bhār* from Mār and *Bār*.

The practical result of this inquiry is the establishment of the Indian equivalents Pahlava, Palhava and Plava for Pallava and Palla, and the conclusion that the names of such peoples, where they occur in the Mahābhārata, Rāmāyaṇa, and other ancient Sanskrit works, refer, in most cases, to Indian tribes and not to nations beyond the frontiers of India, *e.g.*, to the Persian *Pahlavas*. This assumption does not dispute the fact that relationship existed between Non-Aryan races dwelling on both sides of the Indian frontier.

The Paḷḷar, as well as the Paḷḷis, claim to be connected with the Pallavas. The Pallavarājas were in early times already rulers in this country. Some rājas, *e.g.*, those of the Śambhugōtra in the North near Rājamandry still affect the title of Pallavarāja and worship at their marriages the fire and the *vahni*-tree, a twig of which, as we have mentioned above, is used as an arrow at the hunting festival (*Pārivēṭṭai*) on the Vijayadaśamī during the Navarātri or Dasara feast.[65]

In accordance with the interchange between *v* and *m* which has been previously pointed out, the word *Pallava* can be easily recognized in the more modern *Vellama*, *Vellamba*, *Bhillama*, *Yellama* and *Ellama*. The connection between Valluva and Pallava has already been mentioned.

The majority of the Paḷḷar now-a-days occupy the plains, but they have even there retained their innate predilection for the woods and mountains. Wherever possible, they erect their shrines in forests and on hills, and their marriages also take place in such localities. A pandal or wooden shed is there constructed to celebrate them. Before the marriage

---

[65] Read *The Pallavas* by the learned Rev. Thomas Foulkes, and see p. 53.

is actually performed, the bridegroom suddenly leaves his house and starts for some distant place, as if he has suddenly abandoned his intention of marrying, in spite of the preparations that have been made for the wedding. His intended father-in-law intercepts the young man on his way and persuades him to return, promising to give him his daughter as a wife; to this the bridegroom consents.[66] The marriage ceremony is then proceeded with: the Vaḷḷuva priest shows the *Tāli* or marriage necklace to the assembled guests, pronounces the necessary prayers and mantrams, and hands the *Tāli* to the bridegroom, who ties it round the neck of his bride. It is highly probable that the Paḷḷar adopted a part of their marriage rites, especially those resembling the Kāśiyātrā, from the Brahmans. The marriage of the Paḷḷar can be dissolved on either side; the husband divorces his wife by breaking the *Tāli*, and the woman can remarry. Should a wife run away from her husband, she can only remarry with the consent of a pañcāyat. A widow can remarry. The dead are either burnt or buried: burying is cheaper and, therefore, more common among the poorer of the lower classes.

---

[66] This custom resembles strangely the so-called *Kāśiyātrā* among the Brahmans and high-caste Hindus. Pretending to go on a pilgrimage to *Kāśī* (Benares), the bridegroom leaves his house with a wooden stick in his right hand, a kadjan (palm-leaf) book under his left arm, on his left shoulder he carries an umbrella, to which is tied a bundle of clothes, containing also some doll and other necessaries for the journey; his feet are encased in a pair of *pādarakṣa* or hard leather shoes, and on his head he wears a pugri. While on the road, he is overtaken by the father and mother of his bride, who carry respectively two cocoanuts and two vessels filled with water. The intended mother-in-law pours the water over the feet of the youth, while her husband washes them and then gives him the two cocoanuts. Both entreat him not to proceed to Benares, but to return and marry their daughter, to which proposals he eventually listens, and the wedding is celebrated as pre-arranged. The origin of this custom may be that, though every Brahman should visit Benares in order to study there, the young man cannot do so if he becomes a *gṛhastha* or family man. He saves, therefore, his conscience by simulating an immediate departure to Kāśī and manifesting thus his good intentions, which, though not carried out, will be credited to him as if he had actually performed the pilgrimage.

Maḷḷan, *Kulantān*, and *Murukan* are common names among Paḷḷa men, while *Vaḷḷi*, *Tēvānai* (for Dēvayāna corruption of Dēvasēnā) and *Kulantai* (Kulumai) are applied to their women.[67]

The Paḷḷar are an industrious, hardworking, and hard-worked class of land labourers, found mostly in the Madras Presidency, and especially in the southern districts. They toil unintermittingly to enrich their masters, the actual owners of the soil, and they were, until very lately, not much better treated than bondslaves. The time is not remote when the owners of the ground even regarded them as their property, as Helots belonging to the land. Continual bad treatment and exposure to all kinds of hardship have been their sad lot, and it is only natural that this condition should have eventually told on their mental and physical development, but it speaks, on the other hand, much for the superiority of their original nature that, in spite of all the miseries endured, they have been able to retrieve their position under a kinder government and are now starting again with fair prospects of improvement.

The *Pulayar* of Travancore, Cochin, and Malabar correspond to the Paḷḷar in the Tamil country, the Paḷḷar settlers in these countries being often called Pulayar. Their fate resembles that of the Paḷḷar. Constant exposure to the heat of a scorching sun, to the unceasing downpours of rain during the monsoon, and to the violent gales and thunderstorms so prevalent on the West Coast of India, combined with insufficient and unsubstantial nourishment, has undermined and stunted their physique, and their skin has in the course of generations assumed a colour approaching black as nearly as possible. Unfavorable local circumstances have made the position of the Pulayar even worse than that of

---

[67] Murukan and Murukēśan are also names of Subrahmaṇya. See note 16 on p. 16.

the most oppressed races in the Tamil country. The Pariahs or Paḻḻar, who despaired of their sad lot, had at least a chance of improving it by running away from their oppressors without being caught again; but even this prospect was denied to the unfortunate Pulayan. Hemmed in on all sides by mountains, woods, backwaters, swamps, and the sea he could not hope to escape and to better his position; even if he evaded recapture, he had to face death in another cruel form in the wilderness in which he found himself entangled, and out of which he could not extricate himself.

Like the Paḻḻan, the Pulayan, when well treated, has shown himself to be possessed of creditable mental and physical powers. In the census report of Travancore it is said of them that "they are an extremely useful and hard-working race, and are sometimes distinguished by a rare character for truth and honor, which their superiors in the caste scale might well emulate."

The degree of contempt with which the Pulayan is treated is evident from the disgraceful etymological derivation of his name from *Pula*, pollution, as has been already mentioned. Like every other Hindu, the Pulayan takes a pride in his caste and despises, in his turn, all those whom he regards as beneath him. As has also been remarked, the highest class among the Pariahs and the Pulayar is that of the Vaḻḻuvar, who are moreover the priests of the Pariahs and Paḻḻar. This seems to be another proof of the identical origin of the Paḻḻan and Pulayan.

The chief deities of the Pulayan are *Mādan* and the *Fire Pāṇḍavas*.

As a Pariah found at Mēlkōṭa the image of Celvapiḻḻai, as a Śavara was originally in possession of the sacred stone of Jagannātha, so also is the worship of Padmanābha in Trivandrum intimately connected with a Pulayan. Once a *Pulacci* or Pulaya woman, who was living with her husband in the Anantakāḍu jungle, suddenly heard the cry of a baby.

She rushed to the spot and saw, to her surprise, a beautiful child lying on the ground, protected by a cobra. She had compassion on it, and nursed it like her own child. The appearance of a cobra intimated to her the divine origin of the infant. This belief proved true, for the child was an incarnation of Viṣṇu. As soon as the Rāja of Travancore heard of this wonderful event, he built a shrine on the spot where the baby had been found, and dedicated it to Padmanābha. This is the origin of the Padmanābha temple at Trivandrum. The Pulayar round Trivandrum assert to this day that in former times a Pulaya king ruled and had his castle not far from the present capital of Travancore.[68]

This constant connection of individuals belonging to the lowest population with the worship of the Hindu gods is indeed a very peculiar and significant circumstance.

While the Paḷḷar on the East Coast and the Pulayar on the Malabar Coast are mostly agricultural labourers, the *Pulaiyar* and the *Paḷḷiyar* (*Paḷḷiar*) in Madura are on the other hand mountaineers. The former are regarded as the aboriginal inhabitants of the Paḻani Hills, and have been the bondslaves of the Kunnuvar. The Paḷḷiyar dwell on the hills also in Madura and the adjacent districts, avoiding as much as possible any intercourse with strangers.

Related to the Pallas by kinship, and bearing also a similar name, are the *Balla* (Bāla, *Valla*, Vella) and *Bhālla* (*Bhilla* or *Bhīl*).

It is now impossible to decide or explain when and why the original name *Palla* became thus diversified; but after these dialectical variations had once come into use, it was advisable to retain rather than to drop them.

---

[68] The god *Padmanābha* rests with his head at *Tiruvallam* and with his feet at *Tirupālapur* or Tirupādapur. The chief Nambūri priest of Travancore comes from Cochin and is called *Aḻuvañcēri Tamburakaḻ*. See also Rev. S. Mateer's *Land of Charity*, p. 161, and *Native Life in Travancore*, p. 34.

The Ballas.

The tribe which bears this name has become famous throughout India at different times and in different places. We meet the *Ballas* in the North as well as in the South, but their fame is especially connected with those countries which form now-a-days the north-western part of the Bombay Presidency, including its dependencies. Their ancient capital was the renowned *Balabhīpura* in Kāṭhiawār. Enormous ruins, spread over fifteen miles, are evidence of its splendour before its destruction in the eighth century. *Walla* lies now near the site of Balabhīpura. The kings of the Ballas are known as Balla Rājas (Balla-Raos), Balharas and Ballālas. The power and splendour of the Balharas excited the admiration of mediæval Arabian travellers who visited the Indian shores.

Some *Ballas* claim to belong to the *Sūryavaṁśa* or sun-line and trace their descent from Lava's son *Balla*. The bards praise them as *Tatta-Multan-ka-Rao*, the Lords of Tatta and Multan. They called the territory which they conquered *Ballakṣētra* with *Balabhīpur* as its chief town. The Ballas of Surat derive their origin from *Candra* or the moon and connect their pedigree with the Balikaputras, the ancient lords of Aror on the Indus. The present Ballas and the Kāṭhis, like their ancestors, still worship the sun, which is the presiding deity of Multan, a circumstance that intimates a Scythian and Non-Aryan origin. The Ballas are probably identical with the *Mallas* whom we have mentioned above. The Kāṭhi of Kāṭhiawār, who as Kathæi fought against the great Macedonian, claim to be descended from the Ballas.

The name of the Balla Rājas reappears in a different form at a later period in Mysore as the well-known Ballālas.

Many places, all over India, still preserve the name of the Ballas. I reserve this subject for a later chapter, but mention here only such places as *Belgaum* or Baliagrāma,

Ballasamudram, *Ballapallem*, *Ballapur*, *Māblēśvar* (Mahaballēśvara), &c.[69]

The Bhīls.

The Bhīls are probably aborigines of Mārwār. They live scattered over a great tract of country; they dwell so far north as the Aravalli Hills, and they are found in the

---

[69] See Lieutenant-Colonel James Tod's *Annals of Rajasthan*, vol. I, pp. 112, 113: "All the genealogists, ancient and modern, insert the Balla tribe among the Raj-culas. The *byrd*, or blessing, of the bard is *Tatta Mooltan ca rao* (Princes of Tatta and Mooltan), indicative of their original abodes on the Indus. They lay claim, however, to descent from the Sooryavansi, and maintain that their great ancestor, Balla or Bappa, was the offspring of Lava, the eldest son of Ram; that their first settlement in Saurashtra was at the ancient Dhank, in more remote periods called Mongy Pottun; and that, in conquering the country adjacent, they termed it Ballakhetr (their capital Balabhipoora), and assumed the title of Ballah-rac. Here they claim identity with the Gholote race of Mēwar: nor is it impossible that they may be a branch of this family, which long held power in Saurashtra. Before the Ghelotes adopted the worship of Mahadeo, which period is indicated in their annals, the chief object of their adoration was the sun, giving them that *Scythic* resemblance to which the Ballas have every appearance of claim. The Ballas on the continent of Saurashtra on the contrary, assert their origin to be Induvansa, and that they are the Balica-pootras, who were the ancient lords of Arore on the Indus . . . The Cattis claim descent from the Ballas; an additional proof of northern origin, and strengthening their right to the epithet of the bards 'Lords of Moolthan and Tatta.' The Ballas were of sufficient consequence in the thirteenth century to make incursions on Mēwar, and the first exploit of the celebrated Rana Hamir was his killing the Balla chieftain of Choteela. The present chief of Dhank is a Balla, and the tribe yet preserves importance in the peninsula."

Read also *ibidem*, pp. 216–219. "A work written to commemorate the "reign of Rama Raj Sing opens with these words: 'In the west is Sooratdēs, "a country well known: the *barbarians* invaded it, and conquered *Bhalca-nath*; all fell in the sack of Balabhipoora, except the daughter of the "Pramara.' And the Sanderai roll thus commences: When the city of "Balabhi was sacked, the inhabitants fled and founded Balli, Sanderai, and "Nadole in Mordur dēs. These are towns yet of consequence . . . The "tract about Balabhipoora and northward is termed *Bhal*, probably from "the tribe of *Balla*. . The sun was the deity of this northern tribe . . . "The solar orb and its type, fire, were the chief objects of adoration of "Silladitya of Balabhipoora." The Balarājas are also mentioned in the *Asiatic Researches*, vol. IX.

Lieutenant-Colonel Tod's *Travels in Western India*, London, 1839, pp. 147–149, contain the same information as above, to this is added the following: "The Balla pays adoration exclusively to the sun, and it is only in

deserts of Sind and Rājputāna as well as in the woody and inaccessible gorges of Kandesh and Ahmedabad.

The name of the Bhīls occurs in various Sanskrit works, and also in Ptolemy, VII, 1, 66. He makes mention of the *Phyllītai* together with the *Bettigoi* and *Kandaloi*.

Instead of connecting the *Phyllītai* with the Bhīls, as Lassen first rightly proposed to do, Sir A. Cunningham prefers to derive the term *Phyllītai* from the Greek word

---

"Saurashtra that temples to this orb abound; so that religion, tradition as "regards their descent, and personal appearance, all indicate an Indo-scy-"thic origin for this race, and in order to conceal their barbarian (*mletcha*) "extraction, the fable of their birth from Rama may have been devised. "The city of Balabhi, written *Wulleh* in the maps, and now an inconsider-"able village, was said to be twelve coss, or fifteen miles, in circumference. "From its foundations, gigantic bricks, from one and-a-half to two feet in "length, are still dug; but of this hereafter. Enough has been said to "trace the origin of the Balhara of the Arabian travellers, the Baleokouras "of Ptolemy; for, even in the second century, it had claims to the attention "of the royal geographer of Egypt." See *ibidem*, pp. 156, 159–169, where Colonel Tod discusses the Arabic accounts of the *Balhara* princes of India. On page 160 he says: "We may remark upon this description, first, of the "title *Balhara*, that it was derived from *Ballā-cā-Raē*, whose ancient capital "was Balabhipoor, on whose site Ptolemy has placed a Byzantium." I also derive *Balhara* from *Balla Rāja*, the word *Balla* having undergone the change, which I have explained on pp. 71 and 72. Though Colonel Tod gives above the right explanation, he called these rulers on p. 145 "Balhara, or more correctly Balha-raes, exalted kings." The Arabic travellers, especially *Ibn Khurdadba* and *Al Idrisi*, styled these monarchs and interpreted their name *Balhara* as meaning king of kings, and the late Mr. Edward Thomas, of numismatic reputation, explained it to signify *Bara Rai*, great king or lord paramount of the time being. Compare about this subject "The History of India," edited from the posthumous papers of Sir H. M. Elliot by Professor John Dowson, vol. I, pp. 3-5, 9, 13, 21, 24, 86, 87, 201 and 354-358, which latter passage contains a great deal of information on this subject. The *Relation des Voyages faits par les Arabes et les Persans dans l'Inde et à la Chine*, par M. Reinaud; Paris, 1845, should be also consulted.

Colonel Tod devotes a special chapter to *Balabhi* in his *Travels in Western India*, pp. 268–271. "The name of this is now Balli, or Wulleh . . Some interesting additions . . amply confirmed all I had recorded of it (Balabhi) from the Yutis of Balli and Sandera in Marwar, the descendants of those who were expelled on its sack in S. 300 (A.D. 214)" . . Still, both books and tradition connect the tribe of Balla with the ancient sovereigns of Balabhi . . The lord of Balla-khetra would, of course, be Bal-ca-rae, which doubtless originated the epithet, so often noticed, of the Balhara princes . . . Not far from Balabhi, there is a spot still sacred to the pilgrim,

φύλλον, leaf, and to assign to it the meaning of *leaf-clad*. This expression, according to Sir Alexander, appropriately describes the Gonds, though *parṇa*, leaf, is used only in connection with the Śabaras, as he himself admits when referring to them. There is no objection to his explaining *parṇa* by "leaf-clad," though it can also signify "leaf-eating." In fact I prefer to a certain extent the former interpretation of *parṇa*. But as the *Phyllītai* are mentioned by Ptolemy as a

---

and connected with the grand national epic, the *Mahabharat*, called Bheemnath, where there is a fountain, whose waters, in past days, were of miraculous efficacy, and on whose margin is a temple to Siva, which attracts votaries from all quarters. The origin of this spot is referred to the adventures of the Pandua brothers, and their wanderings in exile amongst the forests of Berat, which tradition places in this very region, and its capital, Beratgurh, is held to be the more modern, but still interesting Dholka, included in Balla-khetra; and affording fresh and almost superabundant testimony to the veracity of the ancient chronicles of Mēwar, which state Balabhi, Beratgurh, and Gurh-Gajni to have been the three chief cities, which owned their sway on their expulsion from the "land of the Sauras." The era of Balabhī, which is identical with the Gupta era, begins, according to the correct statement of Albīrūnī, in A.D. 3⅛⅞. The Balabhī grants are dated between the years 207 and 447 of the Gupta era. (See Colonel Tod's *Annals of Rajasthan*, vol. I, 801, and *Travels in Western India*, p. 213, and in the *Indian Antiquary*, vols. XI, pp. 241, 305—9; XV., pp. 189, 273, 335; XVI, p. 147; the researches of Dr. Hultzsch, Prof Bühler, and Mr. Fleet). Balabhī was visited by Hiven Tsiang about 640 A.D. "On its destruction, in the middle of the eighth century, Anhulwarra became the metropolis, and this, as recorded, endured until the fourteenth, when the title of Bal-ca-rae became extinct." (Tod's *Travels in Western India*, p. 214.)

Ptolemy mentions, VII, 1. 83 'Ἱππόκουρα, βασίλειον Βαλεόκούρου,' for which Willberg in his edition of Ptolemy substitutes Βαλερκούρου. This is the passage to which Colonel Tod has referred above in his *Travels* on p. 149, and which is mentioned also in his *Annals*, vol. I, p. 213. Chr. Lassen speaks in his *Indische Alterthumskunde*, vol. III, pp. 179, 185, and 186 of this passage, and places this Hippokura in the south: "Die Stadt muss in der Nähe des "jetzigen Mulkher gelegen haben. . Nur so viel lässt sich, ohne Besorgniss zu "irren, behaupten, dass dem *Siripolemios* die nördlichern, dem Baleokuros "die südlichern Gebiete unterworfen waren." I conjecture that the word *Balla* is contained in Baleokūrū as well as in Balerkūrū, and if the latter is accepted as a reading, the *r* must indicate the title of Rāja or Rao.

About Balabhī consult "Notes on the Ancient City of Balabhipura," by Mr. B. A. R. Nicholson, in the *Journal of the Royal Asiatic Society*, vol. XIII, pp. 146-163. Read also the articles on this subject by the above mentioned scholars, and those of the late Mr. J. Fergusson, and Professor R. Gopal Bhandarkar, in the *Indian Antiquary*, vols. I, III, IV, V, VI, VII, IX, XI,

separate tribe distinguished from the *Kandaloi*, both cannot be merged into one, nor can *Phyllītai* be taken as a Greek word, for Ptolemy does not use Greek expressions instead of, or among other, Indian proper names without tendering an explanation for such an unusual proceeding. *Phyllītai*, moreover, does not occur in Greek in the sense suggested by Sir A. Cunningham.

The passage in Ptolemy has no connection whatever with the Śabaras.[70]

XII, XIV, XV and XVI. Professor Bühler especially has by his publication and translation of a considerable number of Balabhī grants considerably contributed to the elucidation of this hitherto dark passage in Indian history.

Compare also Sir Alexander Cunningham's remarks in the *Archæological Survey of India*, vol. II, pp. 33–35: "We know also that both the Bālas and the Kāthi of the present day pay special adoration to the sun, which was the chief deity of Multān, from the earliest times down to the reign of Aurangzib, by whose orders the idol is said to have been destroyed. It seems probable therefore that the *Bālas* may be the same tribe as the *Malli* or *Malii* of Alexander's historians, as the interchange of the letters *b* and *m*, which is of frequent occurrence in most languages, was very common in the Macedonian dialect." Compare about *Multan*, vol. V, pp. 114–136 of the *Archæological Survey of India;* and about the golden statue of the Sun, H. M. Elliot's *History of India*, vol. I, pp. 11, 23, 27, 35, 82, 205 and 469.

The remark about the Macedonian dialect is misleading, as the Greek historians mention the Malloi, and as the change of *m* into *b* is in this instance of Indian origin.

[70] The *Parāśarapaddhati* mentions the Bhīls, Pulindas, Pullas, Mallas and others in the following lines:

> Pulinda-Mēda-Bhillaśca Pullō Mallaśca Dhāvakaḥ,
> Kundakārō Ḍōkhalō vā Mṛtapō Hastipas tathā;
> Ētē vai Tīvarajjātaḥ kanyāyām Brāhmaṇasya ca.

See Ptolemy, VII, 1, 66; "Περὶ δὲ τὸν Ναναγούναν Φυλλῖται καὶ Βηττιγοί, ἐν οἷς Κάνδαλοι μὲν παρὰ τοὺς Φυλλίτας καὶ τὸν ποταμόν." See Sir A. Cunningham in the *Archæological Survey of India*, vol. IX, p. 151: "In his "(Ptolemy's) day the large district at the head of the *Nanaguna*, or Tapti "River, was occupied by the *Kendali* or *Gondali*, a name which has been "generally identified with that of the Gonds. But their country is described "as *pars Phullitarum*, the *Phullitae* themselves being placed more to the "north. I take this name to be a pure Greek one, φυλλειταί, descriptive "of the 'leaf-clad' aborigines. Varāha Mihira notices the *Parna-Śabaras*, "or 'leaf-clad Sauras'; and we know that the Juangs of the present day "still preserve this primitive costume. I believe, therefore, that there may "have been *Parna Gauḍas*, or 'leaf-clad Gonds,' in the time of Ptolemy, "and that these are the people intended by his Phullitae-Gondali."

The Mârs of Ajmere resemble the Bhīls, and these again are not dissimilar to the Parheyas and Khonds. The Bhīls

This opinion does not appear to coincide with that expressed by Sir A. Cunningham in vol. XXI, p. 93: "Still further to the south Ptolemy places "the *Phallitae* and the *Koudali*, whose country is described as *Pars Phulli-* "*tarum*. Phullitae I take to be a Greek name descriptive of the *Parna* "*Savaras*, or 'leaf-clad Savaras,' one of the most powerful of the aboriginal "races in the early centuries of the Christian era. Their only town was "*Agara*, which may perhaps be identified with Sagar." In H.T. Colebrooke's edition of *Amarakōśa*, Serampore, 1825, p. 252, note j, we read: *śavaraḥ* or *patraśavaraḥ*, wearing feathers (a peacock's tail, &c.). A. Loiseleur Deslongchamps' French edition contains on p. 233 the same remark. In Böthlingk and Roth's *Sanskrit Wörterbuch*, vol. IV, p. 417, stands *patraśavara*, "ein mit Federn sich schmückender Śavara." *Bṛhatsaṁhitā*, XIV, 10, mentions the *Purikadaśārṇāḥ* with *saha nagnaparṇaśabaraiḥ*; and Böthlingk calls *ibidem*, p. 574 the *Parṇaśavara*, von Blättern lebende Śavara, *i.e.*, Savaras, who live on leaves; the term occurs also in Mârkandêya Purāṇa. Some take Parṇa as the name of a people; *e.g.*, Mr. N. Chidambaram Iyor, who translates this passage: *Nagna, Parna and Sabara*. It is possible that in this place three different tribes are enumerated, the *Nagna* (naked), the *Parṇa* and the Śabara: for if two tribes, the *Nagna-śabara* and *Parṇa-śabara*, *i.e.*, the "naked Śabara" and the "leaf-Śabara," are only mentioned, in order to prevent any doubt on this subject, any other mode of expression would have been preferable to the use of the compound in the Instrumental Plural, *i.e.*, to *nagnaparṇaśabaraiḥ*. I ought also not omit to mention that the *Śabarāḥ* occur ten times in the *Bṛhatsaṁhitā*, but only once in the quoted place in connection with either *nagna* or *parṇa*. To these remarks I join General Sir A. Cunningham's comments as contained in his 17th vol. pp. 127, 128: "I think it probable that Colebrooke's reading of *Patra Śavaras* is "erroneous, as Varâha Mihira gives the name of *Parṇa Śavara*, or leaf-clad "Śavaras. Varaha places in the south-east quarter, in the territory of the "aborigines, the Purikas, the Dasâmas, the "*naked Śabaras*, and the *Parṇa* "*Śabaras*," and in the south the *Sauris* and *Kirṇas*. The commentator, "however, takes these two names as one, or *Saari-Kirṇas*, who are probably "the people of Hwen Tsang's *Kirna-Suvarna*. Professor Kern thinks that "the Parṇa Śavaras are 'manifestly the Phyllitae of Ptolemy,' and he ex- "plains the name as 'feeding upon leaves.' But, as we know that the Juângs, "a cognate race, still wear leaves, it seems to me more probable that the "term means 'leaf-clad.' In other places Varâha speaks of the '*Śavara* "savages,' (IX, 15), the 'savage Śabaras and Pulindas' (IX, 29), and "of various tribes of *Śabara* savages (XXXII, 15). This last notice must "refer to more than the two tribes of *Nagna* Śabaras, or 'Naked Savaras, "and *Parna Śavaras*, or 'Leaf-clad.' Both Amara and Varâha date about "A.D. 550."

To my previous remarks, I only add that the term φυλλῖται, as used by Ptolemy, cannot apply to the Śabaras, who are mentioned by him VII, 1, 80 near the Ganges; that a word φυλλειταί does, I believe, not occur in Greek, though φυλλίτης (*m*) and φυλλῖτις (*f*) are used in the sense of φύλλινος, made of leaves: that the *Phyllitae* are distinguished by Ptolemy from the *Kandaloi*

being mostly mountaineers, are called in Kanarese *Koracaru* or *Kuruciyar*, and a Bhīl woman or *Koravañji* is known in Sanskrit as *Bhillā strī* or *Pārvatēyī*.[71] Koravañji is also the name of a girl whom Arjuna is said to have married when he stayed in the *Raivaṭaka* forest.[72]

Cairns, cromlechs and stone platforms testify on the tops of hills to the presence of the Bhīls. Clay horses are, as in Southern India, dedicated to the gods. If images of horses are deposited near or on the tops of hills, the souls of the dead are supposed to shorten their journey to heaven by using them.

Though of a wild and unmanageable disposition and much addicted to thieving, the Bhīls can, when they have once been won by kind and just treatment, be easily turned into useful and trustworthy servants, soldiers, and land labourers. Some of their villages show superior cultivation. In Nimār and elsewhere they fill the post of hereditary

---

and that both cannot be regarded as one nation "*Phyllitae-Gondali*" (IX, p. 151) or as "*leaf-clad Savaras*" (XXI, p. 93); that the country of the *Kondali* is not by Ptolemy described as *Pars Phullitarum*; and that the Śabaras are in the Bṛhatsaṁhitā, IX, 15, 29, and XXXII, 15, not respectively called "*Śavara* savages," "savage Sabaras and Pulindas," and of "various tribes of Śabara savages," for we find there in the text *āvikāñchabaraśūdrān* (IX, 15), *śabarapulindapradhvaṁsakaro* (IX, 29) and *Taṅgaṇa-Kaliṅga-Vaṅga-Draviḍāḥ Śabarāśca naikavidhāḥ*, the Śabaras mentioned, but nowhere as Śabara savages. The *Sāhitya Darpaṇa* mentions the different dialects, by whom they should be spoken, and indicates that the language of the Abhīras and Śabaras should be used by those who gain their living by wood and leaves; *i.e.*, most probably by wood-cutting and leaf-gathering (Ābhīrī Śavarī cāpi kāṣṭhapatrōpajīviṣu). We meet here the Śabaras in connection with *patra*.

Bishop Caldwell advocates in his *Comparative Grammar* the derivation of *Bhīl* from bil, arrow, as he says on p. 464: "*Bhillas*, probably *Billas*, from the Dravidian *vil*, *bil*, a bow, bowmen." The Bettigoi are also called Bittoi, Bittioi, and Bittigoi. Compare Lassen, vol. I, p. 113 (88), and Sherring, vol. II, p. 128-9, 284, 291–300, 326; III, 81–84.

[71] See Dalton, pp. 264, 284, 430 and 439. Compare also "An Account of the Maiwār Bhils," by Mr. T. H. Hendley, *Bengal Asiatic Journal*, vol. XLIV, pp. 347–388.

[72] The marriage is mentioned in a Kanarese ballad. A commentary of the Bhāratacampū goes also by the name of *Koravarāmīyam*.

watchmen, as the Mhārs and Holeyas do in other parts of India.

The chiefs of the Bhīls are known as *Bhillālas.* Some Bhīl chiefs have assumed the title of *Nāyak* or Naick, as the Paḻḻis and Mahārs have done. The founder of the Yādava Dynasty of *Dēvagiri* bore the name of *Bhillama,* which word I have previously explained. This Bhillama is also called Bhillamanṛpa, and Balanṛpa, and Bellam.

Colonel Tod names *Bulla* as the progenitor of the Bhīls.[73]

The Pulindas.

Not only in their name but also in their habits and customs do the Paḻḻar, Pulayar and their kindred tribes

---

[73] See Mr. T. H. Hendley's *Account of the Maiwār Bhils,* vol. 44, p. 347, ff. : " In the hilly tracts, the erection of cairns, usually on hill tops ; the adoption of Shiva and his consort as symbols of the powers of terror and darkness ; the construction of stone platforms on which stand blocks smeared with red paint ; the sacrifice of animals and tradition of human oblations ; the use of effigies of the horse are apparently relics of their ancient faith. Piles of loose stones, . . or mere platforms, are erected on the summits of high hills, . . on these are arranged a large number of stone or burnt clay images of the horse. I have seen a hollow cairn on the verge of a steep crag near Khairwāṛā, four feet in diameter and as many deep, filled with these images, each of which was about four inches in length . . The common explanation of the construction of cairns and horses is as follows :—Heaven is supposed to be but a short distance from earth, but the souls of the dead have to reach it by a very painful and weary journey, which can be avoided to some extent during life by ascending high hills, and there depositing images of the horse—which in addition to reminding the gods of the work already accomplished, serve as chargers upon which the soul may ride a stage to bliss. . . The Bhīl is an excellent wood-man, knows the shortest cuts over the hills ; can walk the roughest paths and climb the steepest crags without slipping or feeling distressed. . . Though robbers, and timorous, owing to ages of ill-treatment, the men are brave when trusted, and very faithful ; they have been looked upon by the Rajpūts as wild beasts to be hunted down as vermin, and are now only beginning to feel themselves men. . History proves them always to have been faithful to their nominal Rajpūt sovereigns, especially in their adversity. The Bhīl is a merry soul loving a jest." About the Bhīls read the account of Mr. W. I. Sinclair in the *Indian Antiquary,* vol. IV, pp. 336–338.

Colonel Tod mentions *Bulla* on the first table of his *Annals.* In the IV Appendix to the same volume on p. 802 *Pulinda-Dēvī* is explained as the goddess of the Bhīl tribe.

With respect to the Naick title in use among the Bhīls, see Dr. Wilson's

resemble the ancient *Pulindas,* who lived in olden times in various districts all over India.

In the Aitarēya Brāhmaṇa the Pulindas, together with the Āndhras, Puṇḍras, Śabaras,[74] and Mūtibas, are declared to be the offspring of the cursed elder sons of Viśvāmitra, while, according to another tradition, they were descended from the dark-skinned, flat-nosed, and dwarfish Niṣāda, who had been produced by rubbing the thigh of the corpse of the impious king Vēna. The Pulindas are frequently mentioned in the classical language of India as well as in those of Europe. The Rāmāyaṇa fixes their abode in different parts of Northern and Southern India. They are found on the banks of the Indus, and even in Ceylon;[75] in Central India they occupied extensive tracts and dwelt among the Bhīls, Śabaras, and Gonds in such a manner that the one are often mistaken for the other. The Mahābhārata, Viṣṇu-, Bhāgavata-, Padma-, and other Purāṇas, the Bṛhatsaṁhitā and various works contain repeated allusions to them, and Ptolemy introduces them by the name of *Pulīndai agriophagoi,*[76] or

---

Indian Caste, vol. I, p. 99: "The word *Nāk*, the contraction of *Nāyak*, is the common epithet (of respect) used by the lowly Mahārs of the Maratha country. From the abundance of *Nāks* connected with the Bhills of the Bāriā jungles, east of Baroda, they are called *Nākadas.*" Compare also Sherring's *Hindu Tribes and Castes,* vol. II, p. 299: "The territories of Baria and Chota Oodepoor, in Rewa Kanta, were infested by a class of Bheels, known as Naikras, of peculiarly savage and predatory habits." Consult also *Indian Antiquary,* vol. III, p. 208, on Nakara; Nāyak; Nayko.

[74] I quote here the derivation of the word *Śabara* proposed by General Sir Alex. Cunningham, *Archæological Survey of India,* vol. XVII, p. 113: "The origin of the name of *Savara* must be sought for outside the "language of the Aryas. In Ṣanskrit *Savara* simply means a 'corpse.' "From Herodotus, however, we learn that the Scythian word for an 'axe' "was *Sagaris*; and as *g* and *v* are interchangeable letters, *Savar* is the same "word as *Sagar.* It seems, therefore, not unreasonable to infer that the "tribes, who were so called, took their name from their habit of carrying "axes. Now it is one of the striking peculiarities of the Savaras that they "are rarely seen without an axe in their hands."

[75] *See* Lassen's *Indische Alterthumskunde,* vol. II, p. 101, 469.

[76] Πουλῖνδαι ἀγριοφάγοι: Ptol., VII, 1, 64.

raw flesh and wild fruits eating Pulindas, as living north of the present Barok.

On Pulaha, Pulastya, Pulōman, &c.

The previously mentioned names of *Pulaha*, *Pulastya*, *Pulōman*, *&c.*, bear in their first two syllables *Pula* a strange resemblance to the name of the *Pulayar* and *Pulindas*. Sanskrit grammarians generally connect the names of these Saints with the root *pul*, to be great, and the word *Pulastya* is also derived from *pulas*, standing for *puras*. These derivations, however, appear too artificial.[77]

Pulastya is said to be the father of *Agastya* and *Viśravas*. Viśravas had four sons, *Kubēra* by Iḍaviḍā (or Ilavilā) and *Rāvaṇa*, *Kumbhakarṇa*, and *Vibhīṣaṇa* by Kēśinī. The saintly civiliser of Southern India, Agastya, is thus, as previously noticed, very closely indeed related to the chief of the hated Rākṣasas, being in fact the uncle of Rāvaṇa, the god-despising king of Laṅkā. While Rāvaṇa conquered India and reduced the gods to abject subjection, from which they were only rescued by Viṣṇu appearing as Bālarāma, his uncle Agastya waged war with the demons and advised Rāma how to subdue the Rākṣasas. Similar family discords assisted Rāma in his warfare against Rāvaṇa and Bāli, whose respective brothers Vibhīṣaṇa and Sugrīva joined Rāma.

While Rāvaṇa is regarded with horror by the Brahmans, *Rāvaṇabhēṭ*, a Vedic work on *Phonetics*, is ascribed to this Rākṣasa. His memory is still cherished by the Jains.

---

[77] Compare the remarks of the Rev. F. Kittel on the root *pulai*, *pule*, *pole* and on *Pulaha* and *Pulastya* in the *Indian Antiquary*, vol. VIII (1879), pp. 50, 51. Though I arrived at my conclusions previously to my reading Mr. Kittel's suggestive article, I admit his priority in this respect and gladly quote his opinion: "The *Pallava* . . and the *Pallavaka*, a libertine, a gallant, "I do not hesitate to connect with *Poleya*; and who knows whether the "ancient Pallava dynasty was not a dynasty of certain *Poleyas* when still a "powerful tribe."

It is also curious that Rāvaṇa is esteemed and acknowledged by pious Paṇḍits as a learned man, and is supposed to have been the author of a Telugu Grammar.[78]

Though the Rākṣasas are described in the Rāmāyaṇa and elsewhere as horrible monsters both physically and morally, it appears that the condition of being a Rākṣasa depended more upon the sins committed by an individual or by his progenitors than upon the accident of birth. If this be admitted, the physical monstrosities ascribed to the Rākṣasas must be regarded as the exaggerated creations of a morbid and hostile imagination.

Even the Rāmāyaṇa extols the beauty and grandeur of Laṅkā, its architectural splendour, and the efficiency of its administration. This latter was so excellent, that no thief dared to pick up any valuable thing lost in its streets. The enemies of Rāma could hardly, therefore, have been so rude and uncivilised as they are generally represented.

The ancient historical capital of Ceylon went by the name of Pulastinagara.[79] If Rāvaṇa is regarded as the king of Laṅkā, and perhaps also as the master of Southern India, and if the present Pulayar are admitted to be representatives of the aborigines, the startling similarity of the names *Pulastya* and *Pulayan* is at once explained.

The relationship between the Paulastya Agastya and the Paulastya Rāvaṇa opens at all events a new and wide perspective. It thus appears that the mind-born sons of Brahma should be taken as the progenitors of all the different races of India, and that, as all men emanate from one common source, no vital difference is acknowledged to exist between

---

[78] Compare the Āndhra Kaumudī in which the *Rāvaṇīya*, the Telugu Grammar ascribed to Rāvaṇa, is repeatedly mentioned.

[79] Megasthenes calls the Singhalese *Palaiogonoi* and the *Periplus maris Erythræi* calls Ceylon *Palaesimundu*. See Lassen's *Ind. Alt.*, I, p. 240 (2nd edition); compare also Mr. T. W. Rhys Davids in the *Indian Antiquary*, vol. II (1873), p. 286, on Pulastipura.

them at first. The degraded condition into which some sank was, therefore, due to subsequent events.

The word *Pula* must be regarded as a corruption of *Palla*. This change from *a* to *u* is easily accounted for. Not only is the letter *a* changed into *u*, as in the Sanskrit *pala* which in Tamil becomes *pulai*, but the vowel *a* is often, especially in the North India, pronounced as *u*.

It is even possible that the names of the demon *Ilvala*, who was destroyed by Agastya, and of his son *Balvala* contain another reference to the original Pallas. At all events the similarity of the names of *Pulaha*, *Pulastya*, *Pulōman*, &c., with that of the Pulayar, as well as the connection which the near relationship between the Sage Agastya and the Rākṣasa Rāvaṇa suggests as existing between the Brahmanical civiliser of Southern India and the representative ruler of the aborigines, should command in future researches the attention of the scholar.

CHAPTER VI.

ON THE PALLIS, AGNIKULAS, PĀNDYAS, VELLĀLAR, &c.

The Agnikulas.

Another portion of the aboriginal South-Indian population is represented by the *Paḷḷis*. The Paḷḷis form at this moment on the whole a highly respectable class, living partly as agriculturists in the country and partly as citizens in towns. They belong to the caste of the *Vanniyar* (வன்னியர்).[80] The word Vanniyan is generally derived from the Sanskrit

---

[80] This caste includes also the Anuppar, Bailagar, Dēvadigar, Kallar, Maravar, Māsadikar, Bantar, Muppar, Nattambādis, Padaiyāccis, Parivārams, Sudras, Uppiliyar, Udayar and Vanniyar. According to the last Census Report the Pallis number 1,300,733 souls, of whom 1,295,049 live in the Madras Presidency, which number is only exceeded by the Shanar with 2,028,546, of whom 1,478,660 dwell also in Madras, by the Vellalar with 1,683,100, and by the Pariahs with 3,223,938 persons, and the whole of the other unclassified population consisting of 3,934,990 individuals. The last two figures refer to the Madras Presidency alone.

Vahni, fire. *Agni*, the god of fire, is connected with the regal office, as kings hold in their hands the firewheel or *Āgnēyacakra*, and the Vanniyar urge in support of their name the regal descent they claim, for they contend that the Pāṇḍya kings belonged to their race. In the north of India four races—the *Cauhān*, *Cālukya* (Sōlaṅki), *Pramāra*, and *Parihāra*—similarly claim to originate from Agni, and are called *Agnikulas*.

The existence of these Fire-races, *Agnikula* or *Vahnikula* (Vanniyan), in North and South India is a remarkable fact. No one can refuse to a scion of a Non-Aryan warrior tribe the title of *Rājaputra*, but in so doing we establish at once Aryan and Non-Aryan Rājaputras or Rājputs. The *Vanniyan* of South India may be accepted as a representative of the Non-Aryan Rājput element. Yet, if we thus admit a Turanian element among the Rājputs, the question arises, how far does it extend? The modern Rājputs of Northern India are in most cases the offspring of mixed parentage, for even Aryan warriors of pure extraction did not scorn in bye-gone times to take as wives by peaceful or violent means the alien daughters of the soil.[81]

The legend goes that after Paraśurāma had swept the Kṣatriya race from the surface of the earth, ignorance and infidelity began to spread again in the land, and the Brahmans were prevented by impious races—Asuras, Daityas, and Dānavas—from fulfilling their sacred rites. *Vasiṣṭha*, or according to others his great rival *Viśvāmitra*, took compassion on the oppressed, and with Indra, Brahma, Śiva, Viṣṇu and the other gods repaired to the Agnikuṇḍa, *i.e.*, the hollow which contained the consecrated fire, on Mount *Abu*, the celebrated peak of Rājasthan. There the hermits prayed and purified the fire fountain with the sacred water of the Ganges. *Indra* first formed a figure of grass and sprinkling on

[81] Compare pp. 45 and 46 on the genealogies of the Rājputs.

it the water of life, cried : "*Mār, Mār*" "Slay, Slay," and the *Paramāra*, the killer of enemies, appeared. Abu Dhar and Ujjain were assigned to him as his territory. *Brahma* instilled his essence into the second image, and throwing it into the pit, *Caluk* or Sōlaṅki appeared with a sword in one hand, the Vēda in the other, and a noose round his neck. He received *Anhalpur*. *Śiva* formed the third figure, and Parihāra rose as an ill-favored black figure armed with a bow. He stumbled and was placed as a guardian at the temple gates. Nine places of the desert, *Marusthalam*, were assigned to him. *Viṣṇu* formed Caturbhuja Cauhān, who appeared like him *four-armed*, in each arm carrying a peculiar weapon. He received *Macāvati Nagarī*. These were the ancestors of the *Agnikulas* who destroyed the *demon races*, and of all the thirty-six royal races the four Agnikulas rank highest, according to "*Chand*, the great bard of the Chohans."[82] This creation "is dated so far back as the opening of the second "age of the Hindus" (Tod, *ibidem*, p. 442). Cauhan chro-

[82] See for this account Tod's *Rajasthan*, vol. II, pp. 440, ff. *Viśvāmitra* is here mentioned as the presiding priest, while in the first volume, p. 95, *Vasiṣṭha* fills this place: "From the fire-fountain a figure issued forth, but he had not a warrior's mien. The Brahmins placed him as guardian of the gate, and thence his name, Prithiha-dwara (portal or door (*dwar*) of the earth; contracted to Prithihara and Purihara). A second issued forth, and being formed in the palm (*chaloo*) of the hand was called Chalooka. A third appeared and was named Pramara (the first striker). He had the blessing of the Ries, and with the others went against the demons, but they did not prevail. Again Vasistha, seated on the lotus, prepared incantations; again he called the gods to aid: and as he poured forth the libation, a figure arose, lofty in stature, of elevated front, hair like jet, eyes rolling, breast expanded, fierce, terrific, clad in armour, quiver filled, a bow in one hand and a brand in the other, quadriform (*chatooranga*), whence his name Chohan (*chatoor* or *cha*, 'four'; *Anga*, body')." About *Canhān*, see Elliot's *Sup. Glossary*, vol. I, p. 63, ff.

The discrepancies between these two legends are considerable, not only so far as the presiding priests are concerned, but also with respect to the order of creation, and because in the description given in the text the gods themselves take part in the creation. *Caluka* or *culuka* signifies a hollowed hand to hold water. Colonel Tod assigns (II, p. 441), as above stated, the *nonāngul Marusthali*, or 'nine habitations of the desert' to Parihāra, while he had previously (vol. I, p. 91) allotted the *No-kote Maroosthulli* to Pramara.

nicles mention *Aja* as the founder of *Ajmere*, the mountain of Aja. Tradition connects Candragupta with the *Mōri* branch of the Pramāras. *Ujjayinī*, the capital of Vikramāditya, is assigned to them, and *Bhōja Rāja*, at whose court the *Nine Gems* are said to have flourished, belonged to the Pramāra tribe.

It is not my purpose to discuss here the fortunes of these celebrated clans; they are only of interest in this inquiry in so far as a connection might be established between the Agnikula of the North and the Vanniyar of the South.

Lassen regards the derivation of the name *Pramāra* from *Paramāra* in the sense of *killer of enemies* as suspicious and ascribes it to a later period.[83] Colonel Tod says: "that "these races, the sons of Agni, were but regenerated, and "converted by the Brahmins to fight their battles, the "clearest interpretation of their allegorical history will dis- "close, and . . warrants our asserting the Agniculas to be "of this same race, which invaded India about two centuries "before Christ."—(Vol. I, p. 90.) No matter whether Colonel Tod's reasoning and conclusion are right or wrong, one can agree with him so far as the Non-Aryan origin of the Agnikulas is concerned.

As has previously been stated, mention is made by Ptolemy, VII, 1, 70, of the Pōruaroi (*Πωρούαροι*), a name which Lassen thinks is derived from Pramāra.[84] I believe that Lassen is mistaken on this point. I prefer to explain the *m* as a modification of an original *v*, as, *e.g.*, in *Vellama* for Pallava, and to suggest *Paravāra* as the original form of Paramāra.

---

[83] See Lassen's *Ind. Alterth.*, III, p. 572: "Da sein Name sonst *Prâmâra* lautet, must jene Erklärung des Namens als eine willkührliche Dichtung gelten."

[84] See Lassen, *ibidem*, III, p. 150: "Von den Porvaroi habe ich schon früher bemerkt, dass ihr Name höchst wahrscheinlich aus dem bekannten, sich *Prâmâra* nennenden Geschlechte der Rajaputra enstellt ist, welcher in der Volkssprache Punvar lautet und in dieser Form weiter von Prâmâra entfernt ist, als Porvara."

I have already connected the Paravārī of the Marātha country with the Pōruaroi of Ptolemy, and eventually with the Pariahs of Southern India. Others identify the Pōruaroi with the Parihāras. Whichever derivation is right, we cannot be far wrong, if we regard the connection between the *Pōruaroi* and the Paravar and Pariahs as established, mainly in consequence of the identity between the Marāthi Paravārī and the Mahārs.[85]

One of the 15 sub-divisions of the South-Indian Vanniyar is called *Parivāram*, which name, if not of Sanskrit origin, may likewise be considered as a connecting link between the northern and southern Paravārī.

Under these circumstances the terms *Pramāra* and *Parihāra* can be traced to an ancient Dravidian source and associated with the Pāradas and similar names. Dr. Fr. Buchanan has, as I have quoted, proposed to connect the Parihāras with the Bhārs.

No doubt most of the Rājputs are easily distinguishable from other Hindus by their proud bearing, fine figure and lighter complexion, but these peculiarities do not necessarily point to an Aryan origin, for such varieties in outward appearance are found in all large nations which contain different classes and ranks. The Turcomans of Western Asia, the Osmanli Turks and the Magyars of Hungary, who are not Aryans, count among the finest races. If the origin of the Agnikulas throughout India can be eventually proved as Non-Aryan, a very important historical fact will

---

[85] *Archæological Survey of India*, vol. IX, p. 5. "The *Poruāri*, who are "very probably the same people as the Parihārs;" *ibidem*, vol. XXI, p. 93: "To the south of the Bolingae, Ptolemy places the *Poruari* with their three "towns, named *Bridama*, *Tholobana*, and *Malaita*. The people I take to be "the Parihār Rājputs, who have occupied this part of the country from a "very early date."—Mr. McCrindle says in his *Ancient India as described by Ptolemy*, p. 164: "Pōrouaroi (*Pōrvaroi*):—This is the famous race of the Pauravas, which, after the time of Alexander, was all predominant in Rajasthāna under the name of the Pramāras."

have been ascertained. New researches have shown that the Aryan population in India is very limited in numbers, and that even admitting all Brahmans to be of pure Aryan origin, this highest caste counts according to the last census only 13,693,439 members against a grand total of 252,541,210.[86]

On the Pallis.

A feeling of superiority has of late re-asserted itself among the Pallis. The Madras Census Report of 1871 states: "The *Vunnias* or *Pullies* are the great agricultural laboring "class of the southern districts. Before the British occu-"pation of the country, they were slaves to the Vellalar "and Brahman cultivators; but a large number of them "are now cultivators on their own account, or else work the "lands of the higher castes, on a system of sharing half "the net produce with the proprietor." [87] With the return

[86] See *Madras Census Report* of 1881, vol. I, pp. 103–105. "It will also be "unnecessary here to go over the old discussion as to how far the caste system "of Southern India is of Aryan origin. It may be safely accepted that the "mass of the people are not Aryan; that indeed none of them are Aryan, "except the Brahmans, probably not all of these, for there are several classes "or sub-divisions of Brāhmans of more or less hazy origin. All the rest of "the so-called Hindus may, if they please, call themselves Shūdras, but they "are in fact a Dravidian or Turanian or Scythian people, who have adopted "in a very highly-developed form, the Aryan caste system, whose germs are "found in the four caste system of Menu . . . Of late years, castes have been "so infinitely multiplied that, even if there were any recognised principle of "precedence, the *nuances* of rank would be so slight, that the places of the "several castes could not be distinguished. But there is no such principle. "Except the members of the admittedly degraded and depressed castes, each "Shūdra thinks, or professes to think, his caste better than his neighbour's. "The Shānār claims to be Rajput. The Kammāla and Pattnūl growl that, if "they had their rights, they would be recognised as Brāhmans. But in this "matter, as in the matter of occupation, modern innovation has had its effect. "Wealth means social pre-eminence in the India of 1881, nearly as much as "it does in England. A Shūdra millionaire cannot be made a Brāhman, but "he can purchase the services of Brāhmans. A Brāhman cannot eat with "him; but this is the Brāhman's loss, for the millionaire's rice is fair and "his ghee unexceptionable."

[87] The *Madras Census Report*, vol. I, p. 157, continues: "Others are simply labourers, and many of them, by taking advances from their employers, are still practically serfs of the soil, and unable to extricate

of self-esteem and independence the Paḷḷis have not been backward in denying such a statement as the one just made concerning their alleged condition of serfdom, and in urging their claims. They have thus lately presented to Government a petition in order to obtain certain concessions at Kāñcīpuram, Śrīraṅgam and Madras. They claim to be the descendants of Maṇimahāmuni and, as what formerly belonged to them, demand the Dharmakartaship of the Ēkāmbarēśvarasvāmi-kōvil in Kāñcīpuram, and the censorship over the nine classes of people there, including in it even the chiefs of the Itaṅkai and Valaṅkai, *i.e.*, of the left and right hand people. The *Jātisaṅgrahasāra* and the *Jātibhēdanūl* contain much valuable information on this topic, though no critical acumen has been exercised in arranging and verifying the evidence.

It is very unfortunate that hardly any question of historical interest which concerns the various classes of the population of this country is considered with impartiality. Class interest and caste pride prevent unbiassed inquiries and even-balanced decisions. The relations of the various agri-

---

themselves from the bondage of the landlord. In all respects, these people have the characteristics of aboriginal tribes. They are, as a rule, a very dark-skinned race, but good field laborers, excellent farm servants, and cultivators. They abound largely in the Tamil districts of Trichinopoly and Tanjore. The *Vunnias*, like so many of the Sûdra castes in the south, are striving to prove that their position in the caste system is a wrong one. In 1833 they attempted, in Pondicherry, to get a legal decision that they were not of a low caste; but the administration refused to deal with the question, on the ground that the Hindu law did not refer to the *Vunnias* at all. There can be no doubt that when the aboriginal tribes ruled in South India, many *Vunnias* raised themselves to the position of *Polygars*, or independent chiefs. The term *Naick* is usually affixed to the names of the Vunnias, and the Naicks of Madura and Tinnevelly were great men not very long ago. There are about thirty sub-divisions of the *Pullies*, named chiefly after their different occupations, but they may all eat together and some intermarry." The Census of 1881, in vol. I, p. 104, says: "The Palli, once the Vellâla's slave, is still working on the soil as a laborer and often as a proprietor. But the work of divorce between occupation and caste has not only begun, but has advanced, and is advancing."

cultural classes to one another are very strained, and the evidence which the one may supply with respect to the other should always be accepted with great caution. Thus the acrimonious dissensions which exist between the Paḻḻis and Veḷḷāḷar are a matter of deep regret, but they must be mentioned here to explain why certain statements concerning both cannot be admitted in an historical inquiry, as they are unsupported by facts and are tainted by prejudice.[88]

The investigation which I am now making is *sine ira et studio*, and I trust it will be accepted as such by those who come within its range.

The difference which at an early stage divided the Paḻḻar from the Paḻḻis was, I believe, that the former confined themselves to the country, *pālayam*, while the latter congregated mostly in villages and towns. These were named *palli* (பல்லி) or *paḻḻi* (பள்ளி) in contradistinction to the country or *Pāḷaiyam* (பாளையம்) in Tamil and *pāḷemu* (పాళెము) in Telugu. The feudal chieftains were called after the country Poligars.[89] The bulk of the Pallas, who lived as agricultural

[88] Compare "The Poyakharries *versus* Meerassidars, or the Revenue System of Madras," by A. Venkatachella Naicker, p. 9. Again, in the third place, Mr. Place states that the Pullees were servants of the Brahmins. Any thing more untrue could not be stated. The Pullees or Vunneers were not the servants of the Brahmins. They were formerly the ruling race of a very large portion of Southern India. The potentates, Sharen, Cholen, and Paundian were all Vunneers, and all the southern and western Poligars and Zemindars are, even at the present time, Vunneers; and on p. 12: In proof that the Pullees or Vunneers were the most powerful and most prevalent race in Southern India, there are the boundary stones which are marked with the Royal "wheel of mandate" an ensign of the royal descent of the Vunneers; also the inscriptions on the temples of Conjeeveram and in fact on the muntapums and other sacred shrines throughout the Chingleput district. Whilst the Vellalars had the mark of a trident on their boundary stones, and the boundary stones of the agraharums bore the impression of a short Brahmin with an umbrella.

Consult about the Śāsanams concerning the Vanniyar *Jātisaṅgrahasāra*, pp. 272, 326, &c.

[89] *Pāḷaiyakkāran* in Tamil and *Pāḷegāḍu* in Telugu. For *Pāḷemu*, encampment, baronial village, occurs in Telugu also the word *Velamu*.

labourers in the country, were, like our rustics, peasants or boors, while the inhabitants of a village or small town (*paḷḷi*, *palli*, *palle*, &c.), assuming the same name as the place they inhabited, became gradually urbane and polite citizens.[90]

The Paḷḷis generally worship in temples dedicated to *Dharmarāja*. In these temples are found the images of Yudhiṣṭhira (or Dharmarāja) and of his four brothers Bhīma, Arjuna, Nakula, and Sahadēva, of Draupadī, of Kṛṣṇa, and occasionally of Pōtarāja (also *Pōturāju* in Telugu and *Pōtappa* in Kanarese). The head of Irāvat, the son of Arjuna and Ulūpī, who, according to popular tradition, was killed on the day preceding the battle as an oblation to the battle-field, and whose head looked on the fight for eighteen days, is often exhibited on a pole during the festival. The Mahābhārata fixes the death of Irāvat on the eighth day of the battle. A Paḷḷi is, as a rule, the *pūjāri* or priest of the shrine. The above-mentioned *Pōtarāja* is a rustic god revered especially in the Telugu, Kanarese, and Marāthi districts, and his wives are known as Gaṅgamma, Pōlakamma or Pōlēramma (the goddess of small-pox), &c.

At the great annual festival in honor of Dharmarāja, or the local god or goddess, people walk over burning coals, in order to testify their purity of mind.

The worship of Dharmarāja is very popular; it is, perhaps, the most widely spread in this country. Over 500 Dharmarāja temples exist in South-Arcot alone. The village goddess is occasionally called Draupadī, and, even where she has a name of her own, she is often merely a substitute for the wife of the Pāṇḍavas. The popularity which the latter enjoy among the lower classes of the inhabitants throughout India is very significant, inasmuch as it is in opposition to *Rāma*, the favorite hero and divine represent-

[90] Compare the meaning of *nāgara* and *nāgaraka*, citizen, polite, clever, from *nagara*, town, in Sanskrit; with πολιτικός from πολίς in Greek; and *urbanus* from *urbs* in Latin.

ative among the Brahmans. It is also remarkable that Brahmans have nothing to do with these temples.

Some of the most celebrated remains in India are those found at the *Seven Pagodas* near Madras. Famous among these rock temples and rock sculptures of *Māmallapuram* or *Māvallipuram* are the Rathas or monolithic temples of the five Pāṇḍavas and of their wife Draupadī. Māmallapuram or Māvallipuram stands, I believe, for *Mahāmallapuram* or *Mahāpallipuram*, that is, the town of the great Mallas or Paḻḻis, both designations being almost identical. And even if *Mahāvallipuram* is to be regarded as connected with the name of the great king *Bali*, he himself, as I have previously endeavoured to show on pp. 14 and 15, should be looked upon as the representative of the Mallas or Pallas, Paḻḻis and Pallavas. If we now associate the cult of the Pāṇḍavas with these relics at Māmallapuram and consider that the inhabitants of this town, the Mallas, worshipped those heroes as do their descendants even to-day, and that the Paḻḻis are the *pūjāris* of these deified persons at this moment, I believe that a relation has been sufficiently established between the Pāṇḍavas and the original inhabitants of this country.[91]

---

[91] See in the *Indian Antiquary*, vol. II, pp. 190 and 191, the article: "Walking through Fire," by Mr. H. J. Stokes, M.C.S. "The situation was on an extensive open plain before the village deity *Draupatī Amman's* temple. The pit lay east and west; the image of the goddess was placed at the west end, and it was towards it that the worshipper walked along the length of the pit from east to west." Vīrappa Vandyan states:—"I was one of the "eight persons who carried the goddess Draupatī Amman to the place where "the fire-treading took place. The fire-pit was a trench about two poles "long by two strides broad. Six babûl trees were cut into faggots and "kindled. Those who trod on the fire were Nachchu, Pûjāri of Periyan-"guḍi, Chidambaram; Pûjāri of Angalamman temple at Achchutaman-"galam; Rāmasāmi Pillei, Stānīka of Draupatī Amman of Periyanguḍi; "Sāminâda Paḍeyāchi of the same place, his brother Subrāya; Subba-"nāyakkan of Vālkei..." Nāgappa Malavarāyan states:—"I live in the next "street to the temple of Draupatī." . . Nachchu Paḍeyāchi states:—"I am "Pūjāri of this temple of Draupatī." The practice of fire-treading is "connected in some places with a legend of Draupadī . . ., the wife of the

In Chingleput and its neighbourhood the Paḷḷis add to their name the title of *Nāyakar* or leader, which term is synonymous with the Telugu *Nāyaḍu* and the Malayālam *Nāyar*. Those in Tanjore and its neighbourhood prefer the Tamil title *Paḍaiyācci* (படையாச்சி),[92] army-leader, which has the same meaning as Nāyakar; while others in Coimbatore, Salem, North and South-Arcot call themselves, like the neighbouring hill men, *Kauṇḍar* (கௌண்டர் or கவுண்டர்). I connect this word with the root *ko*, and derive it from *koṇḍa*, mountain, and if this etymology is right, it shows that these Paḷḷis have preserved in their name some recollection of their original habitat.

Pāṇḍavas."—I have mentioned the names of the worshippers, in order to prove that they are Paḷḷis (Nāyakar) and Paḍaiyāccis.

Read also "The Village Feast," by Captain J.S.F. Mackenzie in the *Indian Antiquary*, vol. III, pp. 6–9, and "Passing through Fire," by Mr. M. J. Walhouse, late M.C.S., in the *Indian Antiquary*, vol. VII., pp. 126–129: "When not done in discharge of vows made in time of sickness or disaster, "the fire-walking seemed to be performed (generally in March and June) in "most places in honour of Vīrabhadra, the portentous flame-clad progeny "of Śiva, who is especially feared as presiding over family discord and mis-"fortune, or else of Dharmarāja, the elder Pāṇḍava, to whom there are five "hundred temples in South Arkaṭ alone, and with whom and Draupadī the "ceremony has some particular association. In Ganjam and Maisūr it is per-"formed in honour of a village goddess, and everywhere seems connected "with aboriginal rites and Śiva-worship, Brāhmaṇs always disowning it." I myself witnessed this fire-treading in June 1885 in Coimbatore. With respect to the sun worship previously mentioned on p. 62 as peculiar to the Scythians, it should be remembered that Draupadī prayed twice to the sun god for assistance. Concerning the explanation of Mahāmallapura I may also add that I regard *Mallapura* as the original form of Mailapur in Madras. These names will be considered in the last part of this treatise.

92 The higher castes are often anxious to enhance their superiority at the expense of their inferiors, whom they ridicule. To this tendency must be ascribed many expressions which reflect on the language used by Pariahs, Paḷḷar, Paḷḷis, and Paḍaiyāccis. The word Paḍaiyācci is derived from *paḍai* and *āṭci*, which originally signified *Army ruling*. Its more correct spelling is Paḍaiyāṭci, படையாட்சி.

The Rev. Mr. Löventhal of Vellore informs me that the hill-people near Vellore insist on being addressed as *Gauṇḍan* and *Gauṇḍaḷ*, and that they feel insulted when called *Ayya* or *Amma*. He tells me also that many Paḷḷis adopt now the title Mudaliyār. Occasionally the term Kauṇḍar is used by Pulayar and Caṇḍālas.

The few necessaries which in India suffice to sustain life, the simplicity of manners, and similarity of external wants create a great uniformity in the habits and mode of living among the population. In this respect there is less difference, perhaps, between the rich and the poor in India than elsewhere. The dwelling places are pretty much the same in villages as in towns, and architectural ambition displays itself mostly in the erection of the temples devoted to the gods, or the palaces occupied by the kings. Difference in population —irrespective of caste, religion, and occupation—forms, therefore, in India the most striking distinction between village and town. In these circumstances even speech does not, as a rule, distinguish between them, and in the Dravidian languages the same expressions *paḻḻi* (*palli*, *haḻḻi*, *&c.*) and *ūr* (*ūru*, &c.) are applied both to village and town.

Different meanings of the word Palli.

The word *Palli* has also various other meanings. In towns, and even in small villages, where people congregate in greater numbers, such buildings and institutions as temples and schools are more easily and more appropriately founded than in a lonely and sparsely populated country. These establishments are accordingly called after the place in which they are erected. The Buddhist and Jain missionaries were probably the first preachers and religious teachers who devoted themselves to the indigenous population and who succeeded in their efforts to win by their sympathy the affection of the masses. This may be the reason why a temple, more particularly if Buddhistic and Jaina, is called *paḻḻi*.

Everything connected with royalty has the term *paḻḻi* prefixed to it in Malayālam as *paḻḻikōvilakam*, a royal palace, *paḻḻimetta*, a royal bed, *paḻḻivāḷ*, a royal sword, *paḻḻivēṭṭa*, a royal chase, &c.[93] This expression is very peculiar indeed,

[93] In Tamil the word *paḻḻi* is at times also used in the sense of *royal*, thus *paḻḻiyaṟai*, like the Malayālam *paḻḻiyaṟa*, denotes the royal bed-chamber,

and seems to prove that the recollection of the splendour and power of the ancient *Pallas* or *Paḻḻis* had not died out in the minds of the people when these words came into use.

The Buddhist missionaries, who propagated throughout India the precepts of their master, spoke and wrote a Prākritised form of Sanskrit. This became gradually the sacred language of the Buddhists, and from India it was, together with the Buddhistic faith, introduced into Ceylon. Though this idiom differed widely from the language which the Dravidian Pallas spoke in those days, in the same way as the priestly Latin differed much from the vernaculars of Northern Europe into which it spread with the progress of Christianity, yet, as the Buddhistic religion came to Ceylon from the country inhabited mostly by Pallas, or in whose towns and temples—*Paḻḻi* or *Pāḷi*—it had found a firm abode, the dialect in which the sacred books reached Ceylon was likewise called *Pāli* after them.

EXPLANATION OF THE WORDS PĀṆḌYA, VELLĀLA, BALLĀLA, BHILLĀLA.

The Paḻḻar and Paḻḻis claim, as has been previously pointed out, kinship with the kings who ruled over them, *i.e.*, with the Pāṇḍyas and Pallavas. It has been proved that a philological connection can be established between the words *Palla*, *Palli* and *Pallava*, and no great difficulty will be experienced in extending it to the name of the Pāṇḍyas.

The *Pāṇḍyas* of Southern India have been linked by legends with the Pāṇḍavas of the North. According to the Harivaṁśa (XXXII, 123), *Pāṇḍya*, together with *Kērala*, *Kōla*, and *Cōla*, was a descendant of the famous king *Duṣyanta*, the husband of Śakuntalā and father of Bharata. *Arjuna* meets and fights in his adventures for the Aśvamēdha with

---

while *paḍukkaiyaṟai* is the common sleeping room. Compare also about *paḻḻi* in the sense of a royal title the *Jātisaṅgrahasāra*, p. 281.

his son *Babhruvāhana*, the king of Maṇipura, which place I have identified with Madura.[94]

The legend of the king Vijaya of Laṅkā is likewise mysteriously and intimately connected with the Pāṇḍavas. He is reported to have wedded a daughter of the Pāṇḍava king of the southern Mathurā, and, as he had from her no offspring, to have invited his nephew from the Indian continent to become his successor. This nephew, *Pāṇḍuvaṁśadēva*, married, in his turn, the princess Bhadrakāñcanā, the daughter of *Pāṇḍu-Śākya* and grand-cousin of Buddha, who had drifted in a boat with her 32 lady companions to Laṅkā and arrived providentially just in time to marry the king.[95]

But there exist also other legends which do not mention this connection between the Pāṇḍavas of the North and the Pāṇḍyas in the South. Among these is one which ascribes the colonisation and civilisation to a northern *Veḻḻaḻan* named *Madura Pāṇḍiyan*, who, on his pilgrimage to Rāmēśvara, observed the great fertility of the *Daṇḍaka* forest and determined to settle in it. He returned to his own town, came back to the South with his family and dependents, cleared the country and erected on the banks of the *Vaikai* river his capital, which he called after himself Madura. The neighbouring Maṟavar assisted him much in the cultivation of the country and foundation of his capital. *Madura Pāṇḍiyan* ruled according to this account 50 years after his arrival, and died 90 years old. He was succeeded by his son *Candrapāṇḍiyan*, who reigned 40 years. *Malayadvajapāṇḍiyan* and *Alakapāṇḍiyan* are mentioned as the next kings.[96]

---

[94] See my monograph "On the Weapons of the Ancient Hindus," pp. 145-152.

[95] See Lassen's *Ind. Alterth.*, vol. II, pp. 95-111.

[96] See "Historical Sketch of the Kingdom of Pāndya," by Horace Hayman Wilson, in the *Journal of the Royal Asiatic Society of G. B. and I.*, vol. III, pp. 199–242, 1836, reprinted in the *Madras Journal of Literature and Science*, vol. VI, pp. 176-216, and H. H. Wilson's Supplementary Note in the *Madras Journal*, vol. VI, pp. 217–220. Compare also Rev. William Taylor's *Oriental Historical Manuscripts*, Madras, 1835, in two volumes; and

Though some have proposed to derive the name *Pāṇḍya*

---

his *Observations on Professor Wilson's Historical Sketch* in the same volume of the *Madras Journal*, pp. 142–157. H. H. Wilson had said in the *Royal Asiatic Society's Journal*, vol. III, p. 201, and in the *Madras Journal*, vol. VI, p. 177, that "an adventurer, named Pândya, of the Velâlar or "agricultural tribe, first established himself in that portion of the south to "which his name was afterwards assigned." See also Wilson's *Mackenzie Collections*, Introduction, p. 45, and *Tamul Books*, p. 203 (new edition).

The Rev. W. Taylor took exception to these statements in his *Oriental Historical Manuscripts*, vol. II, pp. 73, 74, and its Appendix, pp. 35 and 39, and animadverted on Wilson's want of acquaintance with the Tamil language (p. 63), to which charges Wilson replied in his *Supplementary Note*. The Rev. W. Taylor admitted the error of indulging in strong language, but maintained (on p. 144) that: "*Vada dêsattilulla pândiyan-*" *âkira vellâzhan* might have been still better and more accurately rendered "an ancient agriculturist in (or of) the north country," and (on p. 149) that "there is, however, throughout no mention of this person's proper name." In both those statements Taylor is not quite correct. *Ākira* means here "called," for in the same manuscript occur repeatedly such phrases as *Irāmanākirairācā*, the king called Râma, or *Sītaiyākira peṇcāti*, the wife called Sîtâ.

The Tamil manuscript in question is the *Pāṇṭiyamaṇṭalam Cōḻamaṇṭalam pūrvikarājācaritravoḻunku* in the Government Oriental Manuscript Library No. 241, in Wilson's *Mackenzie Collections*, Tamil Local History No. 4, and in W. Taylor's *Catalogue Raisonné*, vol. III, p. 88, No. 2322. On p. 4a the *pāṇḍiyan* is first mentioned as follows: அப்படியே வடதேசத்திலுள்ள பாண்டியனாகிற வெள்ளாளனிந்த ராமேசுராயாத்திரைக்குப்புறப் பட்டு வந்தான் (Appaṭiye vaṭatēcattil uḷḷa Pāṇṭiyan ākiṟa Veḷḷāḷan inta Rāmēcurayāttiraikku puṟappaṭṭu vantān). The translation of which sentence is: "Thus having started came on a pilgrimage to Rāmēśvara a Veḷḷāḷan named Paṇḍiya, who lived in the northern country." Again on p. 5 b: இப்படி.... யரசன் பாண்டியன் பேர் மதுரநாயக பாண்டியன் அவன் முதலுண்டு பண்ணின பட்டணத்துக்குத்தன் பேரைத்தானே வைத்து மதுராபுரி யென்றும் மதுரைநகரென்றும் பேரிட்டு பின்னும் மநேகப் பட்டணங்களையுமுண்டு பண்ணினான் (Ippaṭi.. yaracan Pāṇṭiyan pēr Maturanāyaka Pāṇṭiyan avan mutal uṇṭu paṇṇina paṭṭaṇattukku tan pērai tanē vaittu Maturāpuri yenṟum Maturainakarenṟum pēriṭṭu pinnum anēkappaṭṭaṇaṅkalaiyum uṇṭu paṇṇinān); or in English: Thus this Paṇḍiya king, called Maturapaṇḍiyan, having given to the town he founded first his own name, and having named it Maturāpuri or Maturainagar, established afterwards many towns." The founder of the Coḷa kingdom, *Tiyamān Naḷḷi*, is also called a Veḷḷāḷan, see p. 6 b. Compare Lassen's *Indische Alterth.*, vol. II, p. 108. Mr. J. H. Nelson remarks in his *Manual of Madura*, Part III, p. 44: "The story of the man of Oude may doubtless be found in certain Hindû writings, but I do not believe it is traditional in the country to which it relates. And the Pândya kings of the lunar race are commonly believed to be of the Kshatriya, not of the Vellâla or any

directly from Pāṇḍu and some have ventured other explanations, I believe that none are generally accepted as correct.[97]

I do not flatter myself that I have solved the difficulty, but merely hazard a new conjecture. I suggest that the word *Pāṇḍi* (பாண்டி), which is specially applied to the ancient kingdom of Madura, and the term *Pāṇḍiyan* (பாண்டியன்), which denotes the king who ruled over it, the *Pandiōn*, *Πανδίων* of Ptolemy, VII, 1, 11, are contracted forms for *Paḻḻāṇḍi* and *Paḻḻāṇḍiyan.* The king of Madura, the Perumāl of the Pāṇḍiyas, was regarded as the most powerful king of Southern India, and as such he might well have been named after the people over whom he ruled. The word *Paḻḻāṇḍiyan*, the king of the Pallas, was contracted into Pāṇḍiyan as Tiruvaḻḻaṅkōḍu has become *Tiruvāṅkōḍu*, &c.[98] *Āṇḍi* (ஆண்டி) and *āṇḍavan* (ஆண்டவன்), ruler, come from

agricultural caste." Compare also Part II, p. 31. Already the Rev. W. Taylor has pointed out that Oude is not mentioned as Pāṇḍya's, but only as Rāma's home. Whatever is the right extraction of the Veḻḻāḻar, they as well as their Telugu relatives, the Velamas, regard themselves as Kṣatriyas. The Rev. J. F. Kearns in *The Tribes of South India*, Madras, 1860, alludes to the tradition that the Reddies of Tinnevelly derive their origin from Oude, for he says on p. 8: "There is, however, a circumstance connected with the Reddies which in some degree appears to impart an air of probability at least to the legend, namely, all the Reddies in the province style themselves *Oude* Reddies, and assert that Oude is the native country of their tribe."

[97] Compare Lassen's *Ind. Alterth.*, vol. II, p. 102, and Bishop Caldwell's Introduction to his *Comparative Dravidian Grammar*, p. 16: "The Sanskrit Pāṇḍya is written in Tamil Pāṇḍiya, but the more completely Tamilised form Pāṇḍi is still more commonly used all over Southern India. I derive *Pāṇḍi* not from the Tamil and Malayāḷam *paṇḍu*, ancient, though that is a very tempting derivation, but—as native scholars always derive the word—from the Sanskrit *Pāṇḍu*, the name of the father of the Pāṇḍava brothers. This very form *Pāṇḍya*, in the sense of a descendant of Pāṇḍu, is mentioned, as I am informed by Professor Max Müller, by Kātyāyana, the immediate successor of Pāṇini."

[98] Compare *A History of Travancore*, by P. Shungoonny Menon, p. 2: "Thiruvancodo instead of Sreevalumcode." *Tiruviḍāṅkōḍu* is a wrong conjecture.

Not far from Tiruvaḻḻaṅkōḍu lies *Vaḻḻavaṅkōḍu*, both localities being intimately connected with each other in the history of Travancore. I have also strong reasons to suppose that the name of *Tiruvāṅgāḍu* near Tellicherry is the same as that of *Tiruvalaṅgāḍu* near Calicut. Both places have celebrated temples. That of the latter belongs to the Zamorin. I regard the usual

the Dravidian root *āḷ*, to rule. If we admit that names in common use are more subject to change than other words, the alteration from *āṇḍavan* to *āṇḍiyan* can be easily accounted for. Yet even this modification is not absolutely necessary, as *āṇḍiyan* can also be formed by adding the pronominal affix *an* to *āṇḍi*.[99]

The root *āḷ* is also used in the formation of other similar words, *e.g.*, in *Vāḻḻāḷa* (*Veḻḻāḷa*), *Ballāḷa*, *Bhillāḷa*, &c., and indicates a person of influence among or a lord of the Vallas, Ballas, and Bhillas, which names were originally identical with the name of the Pallas.

The *Veḻḻaḷan* is thus the territorial lord of the despised Paḻḻan, and though both were originally intimately connected with each other, the institution of caste seems to have parted them for good. The relation of the Paḻḻan to the Veḻḻāḷan was that of serf to the owner of the soil, like what existed in Russia, where both, serf and master, belong to the same nation. The abbreviated form of Veḻḻāḷan is Veḻḻāḷ. It is dialectically changed in Kanarese into *Bellāḷ* and is applied to the landowning agriculturist of Kanara. The Toda words *Pālāḷ*, the milkman or priest, and *Kāvilāḷ*, herdsman, are similarly formed. Veḻḻāḷan is also contracted into Veḻḻān.

---

derivation of *vala* in Tiruvalaṅgaḍu from the Sanskrit word *valaya*, bracelet, and the legend connected with this *valaya* as a later invention.

Some time ago advised by a friend I visited *Gūḍuvāñcēri*, a small station on the South-Indian Railway, between Pallavaram and Chingleput, in search of some old tombs. Nobody in Gūḍuvāñcēri was acquainted with these remains. I found them on the slope of a hill near the hamlet *Vallañcēri*, whence the old now deserted village Paḻḻañcēri was pointed out to me. I was further told that Gūḍuvāñcēri was formerly called Putuvāñcēri or New Vāñcēri. In this case Vañcēri should be regarded as a contraction of Vaḻḻañcēri.

Sir A. Cunningham identifies in vol. IX, p. 56 of the *Arch. Surv. of India*, *Bāndogarh* with the *Balantipurgon* of Ptolemy; and this derivation is repeated in vol. XXI, p. 92: "Mr. Carlleyle also suggests that Ptolemy's "fort of Balantipurgon, which I have identified with Bando-garh, may have "derived its name from the Bālands."

[99] See *note* 16 about Subrahmaṇya being called *Paḻani Āṇḍi* or *Paḻani Āṇḍavar*.

As the Veḻḻāḷar are essentially agriculturists and live upon the produce which they derive from cultivation, agriculture is called in Tamil and in Malayālam *veḻḻāṇmai* or *veḻḻāyma*. The Tamil word *Veḻḻāṇmai* is a compound of *Veḻḻaḷ* and *mai*, the affix indicating abstract nouns. It means Veḻḻāḷanship or the occupation and position of a Veḻḻāḷan or cultivator. It may perhaps be necessary to add that the terms *Veḻḻāḷan* and *Veḻḻāṇma* are hardly ever used in Malabar, except in Pālghāt, which, as a border district between the Tamil and Malayālam speaking population, contains many Tamil words. It is customary to derive the name of the *Veḻḻāḷan* from *veḻḻāṇmai*, *i.e.*, the name of the cultivator from the work of cultivation to which he is devoted, but I regard this explanation as erroneous. The Telugu representative of the Tamil *Veḻḻāḷan* is the *Velama* (Vellama), and if *veḻḻāṇmai*, agriculture, were derived from a common Dravidian root, a representative of this word should be found in all or most Dravidian languages. It is most probably not indigenous in Malayālam, nor does it exist in Telugu, where we find words like *kāpu* denote a cultivator and *sāgu* cultivation. The *Velama* is the baron, the *grand-seigneur*, in the Telugu country. Most of the Telugu Rājas belong to the Velama caste. The identity of Velama and Pallava has been already established by me. The *Veḻḻāḷar* of Malabar are called *Nāyar*, which word means, as we have seen, *ruler*. This circumstance is very significant, as the term Veḻḻāḷan, according to my explanation, designates also a ruler.[100]

---

[100] The derivation of *Veḻḻāṇmai* is very uncertain. The Tamil paṇḍits propose different explanations, a sure indication of their uncertainty. Some derive the word from *vēḻ*, benefit, and wish to write it accordingly *Vēḻāṇmai*; others prefer *Veḻḻam*, abundance, &c. The Veḻḻāḷar are cultivators. Cultivation is in India generally divided into *dry* cultivation, which is applied in higher levels and in places which depend entirely on the rainfall, and into *wet* cultivation, which is carried on by means of *irrigation* chiefly from tanks. These two kinds of cultivation are called in Tamil *puncey* (or *puñcai*) and *nancey* (நன்செய் or *nañcey*). in Telugu *meṭṭa* and *pallam* from *pallam*, plain, and in Kanarese *beṭṭa* and *haḻḻa*. *Pul* and *nal* mean bad and good: *puñcey* is a sterile field for dry grains and *nañcey* a

The name of the Ballālas is well known by the dynasty which brought it into prominence, and to which I have alluded previously.

---

rice field. The Telugu and Kanarese expressions denote high land and low land. The high land for want of irrigation produces generally poorer crops than the well-irrigated low land. *Veḻḻam* in Tamil, *Velluva* in Telugu, and *Boḻḻa* in Tulu denote as in the other Dravidian languages *flood* and *inundation*. No inundation can be without water, and in Malayalam *Veḻḻam* seems to mean also water, but this appears not to be the case in Tamil and Telugu. Mr. Nelson has in his laborious *Manual of Madura* first proposed to derive *Veḻḻāṇmai* from veḻḻam and *āṇmai*. He says in Part II, p. 31: "The Tamil "mode of spelling the word Vellālan is வெள்ளாளன் ; and as Vellānmei, "வெள்ளாண்மை, is the word commonly used to express the act of "cultivating (strictly, ruling or managing irrigation), it is but natural to "infer that Vellalan means a cultivator or irrigator of rice fields, rather "than a man of a particular tribe or country." This derivation has been accepted by some authors, generally without giving Mr. Nelson credit for it; but it is not known to the Tamil paṇḍits whom I have consulted, and is repudiated by them. Dr. Gundert, who gives in his *Malayâlam and English Dictionary water* as a meaning of *veḻḻam*, does not connect it with the word *veḻḻāṇmai* which he places under *veḻḻan*, a true man. *Veḻḻāṇmai* is also in Dr. Winslow's *Tamil and English Dictionary* not derived from "*veḻḻam* an inundation, a flood, a deluge, a strong current." It cannot be denied that it is grammatically possible to derive *veḻḻāṇmai* from *veḻḻam* and *āṇmai*, but as *veḻḻāṇmai* in this sense denotes only wet cultivation or irrigation, and the Veḻḻāḻan, as every agriculturist uses both dry and wet cultivation, this name would be inappropriate if applied to him. Curiously enough dry cultivation prevails, if I am not wrongly informed, in the wet districts on the West Coast of South India where, owing to the heaviness of the rain, no tank irrigation is necessary. The derivation from Paḻḻan and *āḻan* as the master of the Paḻḻar or agricultural labourers seems simpler and more preferable. My conjecture is supported by the Tamil and Malayalam term *Veḻḻāṭṭi*, a slave girl, a female servant. The meaning of this expression has not been explained so far as my knowledge goes, but is clear, if it is considered to denote a Paḻḻa woman, a woman of the servile class (பள்ள + ஆட்டி). In this particular instance *āṭṭi* signifies woman in general, as *āḻ* does also occasionally mean servant or slave. *Āṭṭi* occurs in a similar, though more respectable, sense in *manaiyāṭṭi*, housewife, and *peṇṭāṭṭi*, wife. The feminine of *Veḻḻāḻan* is *Veḻḻāḻacci*. The truth of the saying *Usus tyrannus* manifests itself peculiarly in this case. I may add that even my derivation of Veḻḻāṇmai contains the word *āṇmai* as formed from *āḻ* + *mai*.

The Purāṇa of *Tirukaḻukkuṉṟam* near Chingleput, also known as *Pakṣi-tîrtham*, mentions 24 classes of Veḻḻāḻar. They are generally divided in three great sections in Gaṅgākulatar, Indrakulatar, and Maṇkulatar. Of the 63 Aḻvar 13 are Veḻḻāḻar. Mr. Nelson has in his Manual, II, pp. 27-37 collected a great deal of information about them. Compare also "Notes

The Bhillālas are the chiefs among the Bhillas or Bhīls, some of whom are regarded as the offspring of Rājput men and Bhīl women.[101]

The similar formation of all these words tends much to prove the correctness of my conjecture, and as according to my explanation the meaning of *Pāṇḍiyan* as *Paḻḻāṇḍiyan* in identical with that of *Veḷḷāḷan*, the legend which assign to the *Veḷḷāḷan*, who founded the celebrated kingdom of Madura in Southern India, the name of *Pāṇḍiyan* or of rule of the Paḷḷas, may be considered as by no means irrelevan evidence in support of my theory.

on Castes in Southern India," by Mr. J. A. Boyle, in the *Indian Antiquary*, vol. III (1874), pp. 287–289.

As *Paḷemu* is identical with *Velamu*, baronial village, so is Velar originally synonymous with Paḷegāḍu. About the Vellamas compare R John Cain's article in the *Indian Antiquary*, vol. VIII, p. 216.

[101] Compare also *Indian Antiquary*, vol. III, p. 208, and IV, pp. . and 339.